PREPARE

WORKBOOK WITH DIGITAL PACK

David McKeegan
Helen Tiliouine

Second
Edition

C1
LEVEL 9

Cambridge University Press
www.cambridge.org/elt

Cambridge Assessment English
www.cambridgeenglish.org

Information on this title: www.cambridge.org/9781108913379

© Cambridge University Press and Assessment 2022

First published 2022

20 19 18 17 16 15 14 13 12 11 10 9 8 7 6

Printed in Malaysia by Vivar Printing

A catalogue record for this publication is available from the British Library

ISBN   978-1-108-91337-9   Workbook with Digital Pack
ISBN   978-1-108-91336-2   Student's Book with eBook
ISBN   978-1-108-91338-6   Teacher's Book with Digital Pack

CONTENTS

1 FAMILY TIES

VOCABULARY AND READING
RELATIONSHIPS

1 Choose the correct options.

1 Do you usually see eye to *ear / eye* with your cousins?
2 Did your grandparents *spoil / satisfy* you when you were little?
3 Is your family *close-knit / near-knit*?
4 I'm on *good / right* terms with most of my family.
5 I hope that nothing will *come / go* between me and my best friend.
6 My brother seems to rub everyone *out / up* the wrong way at the moment.
7 I think that family *ties / links* are very important. Do you?
8 Maria's very attached *to / on* her sister.
9 My parents both worked full-time, but I never felt like I missed *out / up* on anything.
10 There are four *brothers / siblings* in that family: two boys and two girls.
11 A typical family *unit / group* in my country is quite large.
12 Are you *on / in* speaking terms with your aunt and uncle now?

2 Complete the sentences with one word.

1 I love my brother so much! Nothing will ever **come** .... us.
2 In lots of families, ... are often very competitive with each other.
3 I rarely .... **eye to eye with** my older sister.
4 Our family is .... -knit – we all get on very well.
5 People with big families may sometimes .... **out on** individual attention from their parents.
6 I don't know why, but my cousin often seems to **rub people up the** .... **way.**
7 Is it important for you to **be on good** .... **with** your parents?
8 **Family** .... can often be stronger than any other kind of connection we make in life.
9 I don't get on very well with my sister, but at least we **are on** .... **terms.**
10 It isn't necessary for parents to .... their children in order to show their love for them.
11 I'm very .... **to** my grandparents because I spent a lot of time with them when I was younger.
12 Our **family** .... is quite small: just my mother, my father, me and my brother.

3 Match the definitions to the words or expressions in bold in Exercise 2.

A annoy someone ....
B allow someone, often a child, to do or have everything they want ....
C united ....
D emotionally close to ....
E get on well with someone ....
F a group of related individuals ....
G when people agree with each other ....
H brothers and sisters ....
I friendly enough to talk ....
J not have an opportunity to experience ....
K the friendly feelings between people who are related ....
L harm a relationship ....

4 Read the first paragraph of the article on the opposite page, ignoring the gaps. Which of the following could be an alternative title?

A Why our relationships with our parents will always be problematic
B How our relationships with our parents are constantly developing
C The influence of modern life on our relationships with our parents

 PREPARE FOR THE EXAM

Reading and Use of English Part 1

5 Read the first paragraph again and decide which answer (A, B, C or D) best fits each gap.

0 **A** opposing	**B** confronting	**C** withstanding	**D** challenging
1 **A** perceive	**B** distinguish	**C** observe	**D** contemplate
2 **A** lone	**B** rare	**C** scarce	**D** sole
3 **A** conclusions	**B** evaluations	**C** deductions	**D** assumptions
4 **A** theory	**B** notion	**C** thought	**D** belief
5 **A** outstandingly	**B** distinctively	**C** significantly	**D** vividly
6 **A** degree	**B** grade	**C** extent	**D** rank
7 **A** draws on	**B** comes under	**C** refers to	**D** stems from
8 **A** transfer	**B** shift	**C** amendment	**D** swing

 EXAM TIP

Sometimes phrasal verbs are tested, as in item 7 in this task, and sometimes just the verb is tested, without the particle.

OUR CHANGING / RELATIONSHIPS WITH OUR PARENTS

According to a recent study, among all the different relationships that people have, the parent-child relationship tends to have the best chance of successfully **(0)** _withstanding_ the multiple pressures we experience over the course of a lifetime. The older people get, the more likely they are to **(1)** _____ their parents as individuals, rather than simply people whose **(2)** _____ function is to care for them. The study found that although negative **(3)** _____ of parents are the norm during adolescence, most children's **(4)** _____ of their parents as real people strengthens **(5)** _____ during their 20s. During this period, parents are also beginning to give up some **(6)** _____ of control over their offspring. Because a great deal of the tension between teenagers and their parents **(7)** _____ teenagers feeling that they lack independence, this **(8)** _____ in parental attitude undoubtedly contributes to their children viewing them in a new light. We interviewed two young people, and asked them to reflect on their relationship with their parents.

IRINA, 19, MOSCOW

I live with my parents and grandmother in a small flat in the outskirts of the city. Although my parents worked very hard when I was smaller, and certainly didn't spoil me, they always played games with me in the evenings, and helped me with my schoolwork when I needed it. Because we live in a small flat, and I share a room with my grandmother, as I got older I did sometimes get frustrated when the adults couldn't seem to grasp my growing need for privacy.

Family ties are very important in my country, and my father is really pleased I make the time to listen to my grandmother – his mother. She's very chatty, and talks to me a lot about her own parents and what life was like when she was growing up. I'm more tolerant now than I was a few years ago, and I realise how much pleasure it gives her to tell these stories, even though she does have a tendency to repeat the same ones over and over again! I'm more interested in them now, in fact, because some of the things she remembers relate to significant events in our national history.

I'm much closer to my mother these days than I was when I was aged fourteen or fifteen, and she seems to regard me as more of an equal rather than just a moody teenager, which is nice. We don't always see eye to eye, of course, but I'm better at keeping my temper when things don't go my way. That makes for greater family harmony. My boyfriend often comes round to our flat, and my parents have always made him feel welcome – they treat him like part of the family.

FEDERICO, 18, ROME

I live with my parents in a flat in the city centre. It's quite small, and I'd love to be able to move out and maybe share a flat with other people my age, but life is expensive here, so I think I'll have to wait until after I've finished university to move away from home. And even then, it may be a long time before I'm truly financially independent. That's a common issue in Italy these days, and plenty of people are not affluent enough to move out of their parents' home until at least their mid-thirties.

I went through a phase when I seemed to constantly rub my parents up the wrong way, and they just seemed to tell me off all the time about things like video games – both their content, which they often disapprove of, and their worries about how addictive they are. Now, we're on slightly better terms, but they're still quite concerned about my lifestyle, especially my father, who in particular thinks I should knuckle down and focus entirely on my studies so I can go to university next year. I argue that I need a good work-life balance!

It's important for my parents that we all sit down for a meal together every day. That's typical of Italian families, but it feels quite old-fashioned to me, and I often end up grabbing some fast food with my friends instead. Not having any siblings sometimes makes me feel like I'm missing out a bit – I think it would be more fun if there was someone else my age in the house. But I'm very attached to my parents, and now I'm older, I understand how much hard work they've done to give me a good life.

---

6 Read the rest of the article and answer the questions. Write *Federico*, *Irina* or *both*.

Which person
1 values a tradition less than their parents do? _____
2 appreciates the way a parent's attitude has changed? _____
3 mentions how something in particular matters to one parent? _____
4 expresses regret at not being part of a larger family unit? _____
5 details some of their parents' anxieties? _____
6 admits to sometimes having been a little impatient? _____
7 mentions having had disagreements with their parents? _____
8 remembers their parents regularly spending time with them? _____

7 Match the highlighted words or phrases in the text to the definitions.

1 often bad-tempered _____
2 not getting angry _____
3 do something often _____
4 start working hard _____
5 annoyed, disappointed or discouraged
_____

GRAMMAR
HABITUAL ACTIONS (PAST AND PRESENT)

1 Choose the correct options.

1 My best friend and I *usually / will* have similar opinions on most topics.
2 Didn't you *use to / used to* say you'd never move out of your home town?
3 The next-door neighbours are *keeping / forever* throwing parties that keep us awake at night.
4 Sara *is working / will work* in her uncle's manufacturing business these days.
5 During term time, my mother was *usually / constantly* asking me if I had any homework to do, and it really annoyed me.
6 Mark applied for lots of jobs, but he *used to / kept* getting rejected.
7 They *used to / would* be on good terms, but they can't stand each other now.
8 Why do you *keep / always* looking at your phone?
9 When we were kids, my brother *was always / would* looking for ways to get on my nerves.
10 I *used to / 'll* go to the gym at least three times a week if I can.

2 Put the sentences 1–10 from Exercise 1 into the correct categories.

A Talking about present habits *1*
B Talking about new habits
C Talking about annoying habits in the present

D Talking about past states
E Talking about past habits
F Talking about annoying past habits

3 Choose the correct words to complete the sentences.

1 When I was little, I was _____ falling over and hurting my knees.
   A forever   B usually   C kept
2 Our cousins _____ to come and stay with us at least twice a year.
   A used   B would   C were
3 Dan and Martha didn't _____ to be on speaking terms, but they are fine now.
   A used   B would   C use
4 I'm completely exhausted because I _____ waking up last night for no apparent reason.
   A always   B would   C kept
5 My parents are _____ spoiling my little sister, but they never buy me anything!
   A keep   B constantly   C usually
6 She _____ gets on well with her twin brother, but sometimes he really annoys her.
   A usually   B forever   C always

4 Rearrange the words in bold to form correct sentences.

1 **speaking we on to used terms be**, but we're not now.

2 When I was in primary school, **would I answer never questions teacher's the**.

3 I don't like it when my uncle visits because **up always winding is he me**.

4 **father his constantly him telling was** to get a job.

5 **usually every accept I invitation party** because I don't want to miss out on any fun.

6 If you want to get along with your sister, **you way keep her up do rubbing wrong the why**?

5 Complete the blog post with one word in each gap.

Me and my brother

It is interesting to see how my relationship with my younger brother has changed over the years. Like all first-borns, I ¹ _____ to be an only child, the centre of my parents' attention. When Leo was born, all that changed – and I didn't like it one bit! The new baby was ² _____ demanding to be fed, day and night. Of course, my mother ³ _____ immediately stop what she was doing and feed him, as a mother should. But it annoyed me. What's more, Leo ⁴ _____ waking everyone up in the middle of the night with his crying. Eventually, things calmed down, and I grew to love him. Now that we're both in our teens, we get on really well. We ⁵ _____ see eye to eye on things, and he's ⁶ _____ making me laugh. However, I do get on his nerves when I ⁷ _____ reminding him that I am older, and therefore wiser, than him.

6 Correct the mistakes in the sentences or put a tick by any you think are correct.

1 My grandmother used not to be able to send a text message until I showed her.
2 Amanda use to tease her younger sister about her curly hair.

3 I'm studying about 3 hours a night these days.
4 The neighbour's dog forever is waking me up in the morning with its barking.
5 When Sam was just a little boy, he would be afraid of nothing.

6 It winds me up that you keep always turn up 5 minutes later than our agreed time.
7 It was used to be much harder to get a bank loan than it is now.

8 Her parents didn't use to let her go out with her friends during the week.

VOCABULARY
PHRASAL VERBS WITH LITERAL AND IDIOMATIC MEANINGS

1 Match the phrasal verbs to the definitions.

1 break off		**6** rip off
2 come over		**7** get over
3 let off		**8** run down
4 count on		**9** run by
5 get on		**10** get at

a cheat someone by charging them too much money
b end something suddenly, often a relationship
c criticise someone unfairly
d not be punished
e seem to be a particular type of person
f have a good relationship with someone
g tell someone about something to make sure they approve or understand
h have confidence that you can rely on someone
i criticise someone repeatedly
j recover from a bad experience

1 ___	3 ___	5 ___	7 ___	9 ___
2 ___	4 ___	6 ___	8 ___	10 ___

2 Complete the sentences with the phrasal verbs from Exercise 1 in the correct form.

1 The president wasn't re-elected because people didn't like the way he _____ his political opponents.
2 It took six months for me to _____ my ankle injury.
3 She _____ the relationship because she realised she didn't actually like him.
4 I've got an idea I'd like to _____ you when you have some time.
5 Marco was stopped by the police for speeding, but they _____ him _____ without a fine.
6 I had to find another place to live because I didn't _____ with my housemates.
7 Saira was annoyed because she had been _____ when she bought a used car.
8 He sometimes _____ as arrogant, but he's actually quite shy.
9 You can always _____ Simon to cook a delicious meal. He's such a good cook.
10 I don't know why you're _____ me – I'm not doing anything wrong!

THREE-PART PHRASAL VERBS

3 Complete the sentences with the verbs in the box in the correct form.

> catch   get   keep   look (x2)   make   put   stand

1 So many things are happening in the world, I just can't _____ up with all of it.
2 She was a spoilt child, whose parents let her _____ away with some terrible behaviour.
3 You need to _____ up to bullies, or they will never stop.
4 Although he's rich and famous, he never _____ down on people less fortunate than himself.

5 I don't know how they _____ up with all the noise coming from their next-door neighbour's house.
6 It was great to see you again and _____ up with all of your news.
7 You got a good grade in your latest English test, which _____ up for the bad grade you got last time.
8 My grandmother was a kind and wise woman who the whole family _____ up to.

PREPARE FOR THE EXAM

Reading and Use of English Part 4

4 Complete the second sentence so that it has a similar meaning to the first sentence. Do not change the word given. You must use between three and six words, including the word given.

1 I promise I will follow your instructions exactly.
COUNT
You _____ follow your instructions exactly.

2 She was given an official warning by the traffic police, instead of a fine.
OFF
Instead of a fine, the traffic police _____ an official warning.

3 I'd like to show you the new timetable and get your opinion on it.
RUN
Can I _____ and get your opinion on it?

4 Rudeness is something which will not be tolerated by me in this classroom.
UP
I refuse _____ behaviour in this classroom.

5 There is no way that the person who committed this crime will escape punishment.
AWAY
The person who committed this crime definitely _____ it.

6 Hardly anybody could follow the news because things were happening so quickly.
KEEP
Almost _____ the news because things were happening so quickly.

EXAM TIP

Part 4 of the *Reading and Use of English* section tests your ability to correctly use grammatical structures, as well as idioms, phrasal verbs and other vocabulary items.

LISTENING

1 Look at questions 1 and 2 in Exercise 5 and underline the key words.

 2 You will hear people talking in three different situations. Listen to the first extract and answer questions 1 and 2 in Exercise 5.

3 Now look at the extract and underline the parts that give you the correct answers.

M: What did you think of it?

F: They're incredible birds, aren't they? Marching 100 kilometres from the sea to pair up and start their families.

M: They're funny creatures. Much more graceful swimming in the sea than when they're waddling around on the ice. They looked hilarious.

F: They're definitely cute. The mating pairs were like married couples – so devoted to each other and their children. I was in awe. They put up with so much hardship; I felt quite emotional watching them struggle.

M: Yeah, I thought the film-makers focused too much on that. Trying to tug at your heartstrings. More propaganda than hard facts, actually. They were trying to draw parallels with human behaviour, as if they wanted to present them as role models of traditional hard-working families.

F: Mmm … like they had a moral message to get across to the audience, rather than just present the information? Yes – it made me wonder if it was meant as a children's film.

M: I don't know. A lot of adults were very enthusiastic about it when it was first released. It won a few awards.

F: It was beautifully filmed, that's for sure.

M: Some of the underwater shots were a bit hard to make out, though.

4 Highlight the parts of the extract that might lead you to give wrong answers.

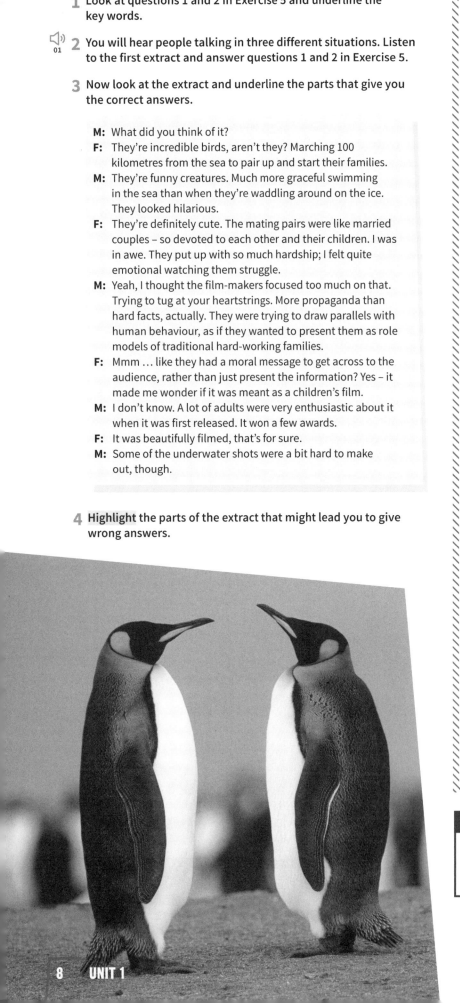

Listening Part 1

 5 Listen to the complete task. You will hear three different extracts. For questions 1–6, choose the answer (A, B or C) which fits best according to what you hear. There are two questions for each extract.

Extract One

You hear a conversation between two friends who have just seen a documentary film about penguins.

1 How does the girl feel about the penguins in the documentary?
 A amazed by their similarity to humans
 B amused by their comical appearance
 C touched by their determination

2 They agree that that documentary was
 A very well made.
 B rather unscientific.
 C aimed at a young audience.

Extract Two

You hear the beginning of a radio interview with a child psychologist called Professor Donna Bailey.

3 How does interviewer feel about people's attitude to him being an only child?
 A surprised at their ignorance
 B irritated by their prejudice
 C reassured that they mean well

4 The professor says that her research into only children shows that
 A they develop in much the same way as other children.
 B the stereotypes about them are justified.
 C they are more likely to be spoilt.

Extract Three

You hear two friends talking about family holidays.

5 The girl loves going on holiday with her family because of
 A the positive change of environment.
 B the feeling of closeness it provides.
 C the opportunity to have new experiences.

6 When talking about family holidays, the boy reveals his
 A desire for independence.
 B regret about his past behaviour.
 C dislike of planned entertainment.

 EXAM TIP

Do not choose an answer just because it has the same words you hear in the recording. It could be a distractor!

READING AND USE OF ENGLISH

1 Read the text in Exercise 5 quickly. How does the writer get on with her grandparents?

A They get on perfectly well.
B They get on her nerves a bit.
C She can't stand them.

2 Complete the phrasal verbs with the words in the box.

> down   forward   out   up

1 look _____ for – try to notice somebody or something
2 look _____ on – think that someone is less important than you
3 look _____ to – respect or admire someone
4 look _____ to – be happy and excited about something that is going to happen

3 Look again at Exercise 5. Which gaps require you to complete a phrasal verb? _____

4 Which gaps require you to complete an idiomatic phrase?
_____

✗ PREPARE FOR THE EXAM

Reading and Use of English Part 2

5 Read the text below and think of the word which best fits each gap. Use only one word in each gap. There is an example at the beginning (0).

My grandparents

Don't get me wrong, I love my grandparents. They're wonderful, and we're on really good (0) *terms* with each other. In fact, it would be true to say that I look (1) _____ to them in many respects. Plus, we can count (2) _____ Grandma to cook a great dinner every time we're there. But there's one thing that really rubs me up the wrong (3) _____ about them. Whenever my brother and I visit them, they're (4) _____ making us put our phones away!

'When we were your age, we used (5) _____ make our own entertainment,' Grandma says. Then Grandpa (6) _____ tell us how many books they read as children, and how much they loved going to the cinema. 'We didn't need phones to have fun,' they say. 'We did other things!'

Yes, Grandma and Grandpa, we know that. But we do those other things *as well*! We're not missing (7) _____ on anything! Unfortunately, this topic is something we will never (8) _____ eye to eye on. Are your grandparents the same?

6 What common meaning do these words have?

> centre   core   eye   heart

7 Complete the sentences with the words from Exercise 6.

1 Everywhere she goes, she likes to be the _____ of attention.
2 The Earth's _____ is about 6,000 degrees Celsius.
3 A disagreement about money was at the _____ of their dispute.
4 It is very calm in the _____ of a storm.

8 Now look at gap 3 in Exercise 9. What do you think the answer is and why?
_____

✓ PREPARE FOR THE EXAM

Reading and Use of English Part 1

9 For questions 1–8, read the text below and decide which answer (A, B, C or D) best fits each gap. There is an example at the beginning (0).

MOBILE PHONES AND GRANDKIDS

When our grandchildren were little, they were (0) *relatively* easy to look after when they came to visit. (1) _____ we did together – be it reading, playing, doing some creative activity – it is safe to (2) _____ that we had their full attention. However, when they became old enough to own mobile phones, everything changed.

Suddenly, those little hand-held screens were the (3) _____ of attention. We would be chatting away quite nicely when a little *ping* would go off, and out came the phone! This rudeness was not something we were going to (4) _____ up with for long. So we established a (5) _____: as soon as you walk through our door, your phones get locked in the drawer.

They accepted it, somewhat grumpily, and now we get (6) _____ just fine again. I suspect our grandchildren (7) _____ down on us, thinking we're rather ignorant when it comes to technology. But we know more than they think. Neither of them is (8) _____ that I have this blog, for example!

0 A roughly   **B** adequately   **C** relatively   **D** approximately
1 A Whatever   **B** Wherever   **C** Whichever   **D** Whoever
2 A tell   **B** state   **C** mention   **D** say
3 A core   **B** centre   **C** eye   **D** heart
4 A stay   **B** give   **C** bear   **D** put
5 A command   **B** guide   **C** rule   **D** habit
6 A on   **B** through   **C** around   **D** across
7 A fall   **B** look   **C** cut   **D** step
8 A conscious   **B** sensible   **C** aware   **D** alert

✓ EXAM TIP

This part of the exam tests your knowledge of grammar and some aspects of vocabulary, such as phrasal verbs, fixed phrases and idioms, and strong collocations.

✓ EXAM TIP

This part of the exam tests your understanding of the meaning of words, their collocations and how they fit grammatically into a sentence.

2 MAKING A POINT

VOCABULARY AND READING
COMMUNICATION

1 Match the words and expressions to the definitions. One of the definitions can be used twice.

1	launch into	6	wink
2	give away	7	put (something) down to
3	assert	8	flick through
4	attribute (something) to	9	raise eyebrows
5	denote	10	reputedly

a close one eye for a short time as a way of showing friendliness
b surprise people
c say or think that something is the result of a particular thing
d tell a secret or reveal something
e said to be true, although it isn't certain
f represent or mean
g quickly start doing or saying something
h look quickly at the pages of a book or a magazine
i say that something is definitely true

1	3	5	7	9 ....
2	4	6	8	10 ....

2 Complete the sentences with the words and expressions from Exercise 1.

1 I hope the expression on my face didn't .... what I was thinking. I didn't want anyone to know.
2 Jana decided to .... some magazines while she was waiting for her appointment.
3 According to David's friends, his success can be .... hard work and an ability to communicate ideas effectively.
4 That tree is .... the oldest in the country.
5 If you .... something as surprising as that, you need to be able to prove it.
6 What did this symbol .... in ancient Egypt?
7 If you say strange things like that, you'll definitely ...., and maybe even upset people.
8 It's a bad idea to .... into an answer before the other speaker has even finished their question.
9 I thought he was being serious for a second, but then he .... at me!
10 The doctor .... my illness .... to too much stress and not taking enough care of myself.

3 Complete the sentences so that they are true for you.

1 I wink when I ....
2 I can assert with confidence that ....
3 I attribute my good level of English to ....
4 Something I once heard that raised eyebrows was ....
5 The place where I live is reputedly ....

4 Read the article on the opposite page, quickly. Which of the following topics are covered?

A how to listen effectively
B how to ask good questions
C why people don't want to listen to each other
D what makes it hard to hear people nowadays

PREPARE FOR THE EXAM

Reading and Use of English Part 5

5 You are going to read an article about listening. For questions 1–6, choose the answer (A, B, C or D) which you think fits best according to the text.

1 Why does the writer describe people's response to discovering she is a journalist?
A to illustrate a point she wants to make
B to explain the reasons for a decision
C to justify her attitude towards others
D to highlight an aspect of her professional life

2 The writer uses the phrase 'some taller than others' in line 22 to show that
A she thought that some people were particularly entertaining.
B she found the appearance of some adults slightly frightening.
C she doubted whether she would remember some of the tales.
D she questioned the accuracy of some of the stories she heard.

3 What does the writer say about listening in the third paragraph?
A It is helpful to remain quiet when someone is speaking.
B It is particularly demanding to listen to intelligent people.
C It is important to focus on what the speaker wishes to convey.
D It is worth asking a speaker to slow down if they talk too quickly.

4 What does the writer say about questions in the fourth paragraph?
A People are more willing to answer good ones.
B Only good ones will lead to meaningful answers.
C Most people are unaware of how to ask good ones.
D Good ones may change the speaker's mind on an issue.

5 The writer suggests that she asks people about their interests in order to
A avoid the risk of giving offence.
B encourage them to give away secrets.
C enable a constructive exchange of opinions.
D have an opportunity to tell them about herself.

6 What does the writer tell the reader in the final paragraph?
A Learning to listen will make life more rewarding.
B Be prepared to explain to others how to listen well.
C Listening to other people can improve memory skills.
D Accept that there are people who may never learn to listen.

EXAM TIP

The questions are always in the same order as the information in the text.

WHY LISTENING IS THE
REAL KEY
TO COMMUNICATION

When people find out I'm a journalist, they typically launch into a story about how they used to write for their school newspaper or that their cousin is a blogger. Or they might say they loved a film about a newsroom, but can't remember the name. It's rare that people don't interrupt and shift the conversation towards themselves. Bad listeners aren't necessarily bad or rude people. You're likely to have a dear friend who's a bad listener. Perhaps you yourself are not the best listener. And you could be forgiven. In many ways, we've been conditioned not to listen. This can in part be attributed to all the loud noises that accompany modern life. Noise levels in restaurants force diners to strain to hear one another. Traffic on city streets, music in shops and the coffee machines at your local café can reputedly exceed the volume of normal conversation by as much as 30 decibels. All this when listening is arguably more valuable than speaking.

I'm a listener by profession, but I'm also a listener by nature. Growing up, I was surrounded by colourful relatives and neighbours who knew how to tell a good tale, often with a cheerful wink (some taller than others, and raising eyebrows because they were so very unlikely). I learned early on that listening to the same story told by multiple sources got you closer to the truth. After a couple of years studying the neuroscience, psychology and sociology of listening, I learned that listening goes beyond just hearing what people say. It's also paying attention to how they say it, what they do while they are saying it, in what context it's being said, and how what they say resonates with you.

Listening isn't about simply keeping quiet while someone else talks. Quite the opposite. A lot of listening has to do with how you respond – the degree to which you help the person you're listening to express their thoughts clearly and, in the process, make your own thoughts clearer. It starts with an openness and willingness to truly follow another person's story without presumption or getting distracted by what's going on in your own head. This can be a problem for smart people whose galloping thoughts may race ahead of the speaker's words, often in the wrong direction.

Good listeners ask good questions. One of the most valuable lessons I learned as a journalist is that everyone is interesting if you ask the right questions. If someone seems dull or uninteresting, it can be put down to you. Good questions don't have a hidden agenda of fixing, advising, convincing or correcting. They don't begin with 'Don't you think … ' or 'Wouldn't you agree … ', and they definitely don't end with 'Right?' The idea is to explore the speaker's point of view, not to sway it. Also, avoid asking questions like 'What do you do for a living?', 'What part of town do you live in?' and 'Are you married?' These don't denote an honest attempt to get to know people so much as rank them in the social hierarchy.

Instead, ask about people's interests. Try to find out what excites or annoys them – their simple pleasures and what keeps them up at night. Ask expansive questions such as, 'What's the best gift you ever received?' and 'If you could live anywhere in the world, where would you live?' Listening to people like this is also a way to bridge differences and find common ground. Once you find out someone can't resist chocolate, whistles when nervous or has a room in their house dedicated to their yo-yo collection, it's hard to reduce them to a particular ideological position. You might not agree with them, but you gain understanding about their background and influences, which is essential to reaching compromise. Moreover, listening to others makes it more likely that they will listen to you. This is in part because it's human nature to return courtesies, but also because you learn people's values and motivations. With this, you'll be better able to craft a message that resonates.

Listening is a skill and, like any skill, it degrades if you don't do it enough. It takes awareness, motivation and practice. While some may have more natural ability and others may have to try harder, everyone will benefit from the effort. The more people you listen to, the more aspects of humanity you'll recognise and the better your judgement, instincts and intuitions will become. We are, each of us, what we attend to in life. To listen poorly, selectively, or not at all, is to limit your understanding of the world and prevent yourself becoming the best you can be.

6 Match the **highlighted** words or phrases in the text to the definitions.

 1 the belief that something is true without having any proof ....
 2 persuade someone to believe or do something ....
 3 make the difference between two ideas smaller ....
 4 make a great effort ....
 5 place in order of importance ....

GRAMMAR
THE GRAMMAR OF MULTI-WORD VERBS

1 Choose the correct options. Sometimes both options are correct.

1 I flicked *the book through / through the book*, but it didn't interest me.
2 My parents brought *up me / me up* to question everything.
3 She walks so quickly – it's difficult to keep *her up with / up with her*.
4 Why are you always running *him down / down him*?
5 I put *my success down / down my success* to hard work and luck.
6 He went to the party dressed *as a clown up / up as a clown*.
7 You need to stand *your boss up to / up to your boss* if he's being unfair.
8 The lecturer used graphs to help him get *his point across / across his point*.
9 If your shoes are hurting you, take *them off / off them*.
10 Do you like *dressing up / dressing it up* for Halloween?

2 Rearrange the words in brackets to form correct sentences. Sometimes there are two correct ways.

1 The teacher _____ (her / off / told / for) chatting in class.
2 What can we do to _____ (Daniel / up / cheer)?
3 I try to _____ (trouble / out / stay / of), but I don't always succeed
4 The police know who did it, but they haven't been able to _____ (him / down / track) yet.
5 _____ (you / checked / out / the new cafe / have) yet? It's great!
6 Can you _____ (the doorbell / out / listen / for) while I'm in the shower, please?
7 I'm going to _____ (in / let / on / you) a secret.
8 Try not to _____ (too much / into / read) what he said.

3 Change the object to a pronoun. Sometimes you need to change the word order.

0 Take off your shoes.
  Take them off.

1 We cheered up our grandfather.
_____
2 I'm flicking through your essay.
_____
3 My boss told off my colleague and I.
_____
4 Always back up your work.
_____
5 Stop going on about your relatives.
_____
6 They tracked the escaped prisoner down.
_____

4 Complete the conversations with the words in A–D in the correct order.

1 A: That was a confusing lesson, wasn't it?
  B: Yes, I found it really hard to _____.
2 A: Here, I've brought you some flowers.
  B: Thanks! That's really _____.
3 A: Have you been to the new skate park yet?
  B: No. Let's _____ this weekend.
4 A: Simon and Gurwinder had a big argument again yesterday.
  B: I hope you _____! It's not a good idea to get involved.

A in all it take   C me up cheered
B it out of stayed   D it out check

5 Correct the mistakes in the sentences or put a tick by any you think are correct.

1 I told you a secret and you gave it along. _____
2 In your essay, you back your argument up well.
_____
3 The official report set this down to human error.
_____
4 They carried working on after the meeting was over.
_____
5 Paulo always tries his best – you shouldn't run down him.
_____
6 There is something I need to put on your attention.
_____

PREPARE FOR THE EXAM

Reading and Use of English Part 2

6 Read the text below and think of the word which best fits each gap. Use only one word in each gap. There is an example at the beginning (0).

My friend's special cat

I was intrigued when my friend Alex came up to me after school and said he was going to let me **(0)** *in* on a secret. 'My cat can see into the future,' he told me. 'She knows when my father sets **(1)** _____ on his journey home from work, and she goes to sit by the window, waiting for him.'

Now, I was brought **(2)** _____ to question everything. If somebody makes an extraordinary claim like that, they had better **(3)** _____ it up with some good evidence! So Alex invited me to his house.

We were both sitting in his living room **(4)** _____, at 5 o'clock, the cat jumped on to the windowsill. Ten minutes **(5)** _____, Alex's father arrived home. 'See!' said Alex, triumphantly.

I wasn't convinced. I put it **(6)** _____ to the fact that Alex's father finishes work at the same time every day, and the cat is just fitting in with his routine. **(7)** _____ this obvious explanation, Alex still goes **(8)** _____ about his 'psychic cat' almost every time we meet.

EXAM TIP

Make sure you write only one word in each gap!

1 Complete the colloquial expressions with the missing vowels.

1 _ll _v_r th_ pl_c_
2 c__ldn't c_r_ l_ss
3 __s__r s__d th_n d_n_
4 g_t _ff _n th_ wr_ng f__t
5 it's _b__t t_m_
6 k__p y__ _n th_ p_ct_r_
7 k__p _ str__ght f_c_
8 kn_w s_m_th_ng _ns_d_ __t
9 _p f_r gr_bs
10 _p _n th_ __r

2 Match the colloquial expressions in Exercise 1 to the formal versions.

Colloquial		Formal
0	*it's about time*	it should have happened earlier
1		available
2		give you all the latest information
3		be totally unconcerned
4		start a relationship badly
5		stop yourself from laughing
6		apparently simple but actually difficult
7		have a thorough knowledge of
8		everywhere
9		not yet decided

3 Complete the sentences with the colloquial expressions from Exercises 1 and 2 in the correct form.

1 He says he _____ about the exam, but I think he's actually quite anxious.
2 _____ they answered my email. I wrote to them last month.
3 Can you _____ about what's going on while I'm away? I don't want to miss anything.
4 We've got a pair of tickets to tonight's concert _____ – all you have to do to win them is answer the following question …
5 Sally and I _____, but we get along really well now.
6 I didn't think it would take long, but putting a new wheel on my bike was _____.
7 Everyone had difficulty _____ when the president tripped up on the stairs.
8 You should ask Maria if you have any questions about the schedule because she _____.
9 I searched _____ for the trainers you wanted, but I couldn't find them anywhere.
10 The final dates are still _____, but we hope to announce them before the end of the month.

4 Rewrite the sentences using a colloquial expression.

1 I'm afraid we started this relationship badly.

2 They went everywhere looking for a nice café.

3 That sounds simple, but it is actually very difficult.

4 I have absolutely no interest in what he thinks.

5 Our holiday plans are still undecided.

6 I have a thorough knowledge of these streets.

5 Complete the conversations with colloquial expressions.

1 **A:** Nice new laptop, Mehdi! It's _____ you upgraded, isn't it? That one you had was pretty old!
  B: I know! I got this on sale at my local computer store.
  A: Are you sure it works properly?
  B: Yes, I asked Tina to check it out before I bought it. She knows technology _____. I'm very pleased with it.

2 **A:** Hi, Soraya. I've been looking for you _____. Do you know if the team has been picked for the match this weekend?
  B: It's still _____, I'm afraid. You'll probably play on the wing again. Is that OK with you?
  A: I _____ what position I play, as long as it's not goalkeeper!
  B: Well, I'll _____ – we should know before Friday.
  A: We've got to win this match.
  B: That's _____ – our opponents are league champions!

WRITING
AN INFORMAL EMAIL

>> SEE *PREPARE TO WRITE* BOX, STUDENT'S BOOK PAGE 19

1 Make a list of the ways you can communicate with friends and family when you're not together.

_____
_____
_____
_____

2 Write two advantages of each of these ways of communicating.

_____
_____
_____
_____
_____
_____

3 Read the question. What would you say to reassure Alex?

> You have received this email from a friend:
>
> … My sister's got a new job in another country. I'm going to miss her so much! I know we can stay in touch online, but it's not the same as being together. I'm worried we won't be so close any more. Do you think that our relationship can stay as strong when we're just communicating online, and have you got any advice for me?
> Write soon!
> Alex
>
> Write your **email** in reply.

_____
_____
_____
_____

4 Read Sam's reply, ignoring the gaps. Are any of Sam's ideas the same as yours?

Hi Alex,

Good to hear from you! Congratulations to your sister for getting a new job, but I can imagine how tough it must be for you – I'd hate it if I couldn't see my brother every day! But **(1)** _____ you do, don't despair – you'll still be able to talk to her, even if it isn't exactly the same as being face to face.

Anyway, **(2)** _____, yes, I do think people can communicate properly online, **(3)** _____ because we already do things like video calls with people we live close to – sometimes even in preference to meeting up in person – **(4)** _____, weirdly, we can often talk more openly when we're not actually in a room with someone.

(5) _____ is that a good long email is as precious nowadays as a long letter used to be for our grandparents. Believe me, your sister will value your emails, and re-read them time and again. **(6)** _____, you'll be able to add photos, too!

And **(7)** _____ to that, you can send her instant messages whenever you like, so she'll always know how you're feeling. I think in some ways, you'll feel as close as ever, to be honest. **(8)** _____ set aside time for longer video calls – you could do that over a meal, maybe even cook the same dishes!

(9) _____ there will be times when you wish you could just be with her and give her a hug, not to **(10)** _____ just hang out, without talking. But remember, she's your sister – she'll always be one of your best friends!

Take care,

Sam

5 Complete Sam's reply using one of the options below in each gap. Add capital letters where necessary.

A you might also want to
B but also because
C mention
D whatever
E another thing I'd say
F not just
G in addition
H in answer to your question
I besides
J it goes without saying that

6 Correct the mistakes in the expressions in bold.

A **So when you want a good tip, it's this**: don't video chat for longer than an hour at a time. ....

B I'd love to talk this week. **After said that**, I'm actually pretty busy until Friday. ....

C You'll be very busy, so you may not miss her as much as you expect. **And in some case**, you'll be able to go and visit her. ....

D **I'll tell you that** – let's chat about it this evening! ....

E You can send instant messages **so well as** make voice calls. ....

F I haven't been feeling great. **But enough of this** – how are you these days? ....

7 Complete the sentences using the corrected expressions from Exercise 6. Add punctuation where necessary.

1 The holiday wasn't as exciting as I'd hoped .... I did get a much-needed rest.

2 .... I'm free at 11, so we could meet for a coffee then.

3 The weather's really been getting me down .... tell me about your new job. I've heard you're doing really well!

4 .... try to arrange a regular time-slot for calls. That's what I did with my brother when he moved to a new city.

5 I know your sister was a bit fed up with her old job .... you said she wanted to live abroad for a while.

6 She'll get useful experience .... learn a new language.

8 Look at the email below. What advice can you give Jo? Make notes.

You have received this email from a friend:

… I think a lot about my appearance because I feel the way I dress and look communicates important things about my personality. Now I've got a job in an office where most people dress in quite a formal way. I know that I don't have to dress like everyone else, but I don't want to upset people. Do you have any advice for me?

All the best,

Jo

....
....
....
....

PREPARE FOR THE EXAM

Writing Part 2

9 Write your email to Jo. Use some of the expressions you have learned. Write 220–260 words.

EXAM TIP

Make a plan before you start writing, making sure it includes all the points you need to cover.

3 WHEN TOMORROW COMES

VOCABULARY AND READING
THINKING OF THE FUTURE

1 Complete the words in the sentences. The first letter is given.

0 When do you e _n v i s a g e_ that the repairs will be completed?

1 Please be patient. A member of our customer service team will be with you s _____ .

2 I don't think that the end of the world is i _____ , although some people claim it might happen very soon!

3 Kevin's job will keep him going in the s _____ t _____ , but he wants to find something better before too long.

4 Her baby should already have been born; it's a week o _____ .

5 Lana is hoping to live here for the f _____ future.

6 The c _____ months are likely to be interesting – I've just moved into a flat with some amazing people!

7 An announcement about the new sports centre is p _____ – they may start building it soon.

8 Buying an electric car before oil prices rose showed great f _____ !

9 Jane can't make any l _____ – t _____ plans until she has a permanent position in the company.

10 When setting up a project, it's good to try and a _____ any potential problems before you start.

2 Replace the words in italics with one of the completed words or phrases from Exercise 1.

1 What do you think you will achieve in the _next_ year?

_____

2 You need _the ability to predict what might happen_ in order to do well in the retail business. _____

3 We promise that you will receive an answer from us _soon_. _____

4 It looks as if a storm is _going to happen very soon_ – let's go back home. _____

5 If you don't pay the parking fine within a week, it will be considered _late_. _____

6 I know what you want to do in the _next few weeks_, but what are your long-term plans?

_____

3 Complete the sentences so that they are true for you.

1 I think that the coming months will be

_____ .

2 In the short term, I'd like to _____ .

3 In the long term, I'd like to _____ .

4 Regarding the future of my country, I anticipate that _____ .

5 One time when I showed great foresight was when I _____ .

4 Read the first two paragraphs of the article on the opposite page, ignoring the gaps. What might the journalist who interviewed Tesla have said about him?

A This man has invented a wireless transmission system that will change the world.

B The statue in San Francisco is a well-deserved tribute to an important inventor.

C It is hard to imagine that what this inventor has predicted could ever actually happen.

 PREPARE FOR THE EXAM

Reading and Use of English Part 2

5 For questions 1–8, read the first two paragraphs again and think of the word which best fits each gap. Use only one word in each gap. There is an example at the beginning (0).

 EXAM TIP

Contractions (e.g. _it's_, _don't_) count as two words in this task, so don't use them as answers!

6 Read the rest of the article. Decide if each sentence is _T_ (True), _F_ (False) or _NM_ (Not Mentioned).

1 Mark Twain was an expert on telephonic messaging systems. _____

2 The name of the Apollo mission was inspired by Jules Verne's story. _____

3 Jules Verne discussed gravity with scientists before writing his story. _____

4 Boyle's predictions are considered more important than his scientific work. _____

5 Boyle worked on practical ways to help people live longer. _____

6 Some of Boyle's predictions were very accurate. _____

7 Da Vinci focused on a narrow range of ideas. _____

8 Nicholas felt comfortable during his jump from the hot air balloon. _____

7 Match the highlighted words or phrases in the text to the definitions.

1 with human beings on board _____

2 a high level of knowledge _____

3 famous _____

4 talented _____

5 sent into space _____

PEOPLE WHO PREDICTED →THE FUTURE

Have you heard of Nikola Tesla? He was a Serbian-American inventor and has often **(0)** _been_ called 'the man who invented the 20th century'. In a newspaper interview in 1909, he was asked what he thought the future might hold **(1)** _____ technology. Guess what he said? 'It will soon be possible to transmit wireless messages all over the world **(2)** _____ simply that any individual can carry and operate his own apparatus.' Given that it was not **(3)** _____ 1973 that the first mobile phone was created, and that wi-fi only **(4)** _____ available in 1991, Tesla's foresight was extraordinary.

In 1926, he made another interesting prediction, which anticipated modern-day video-calling: 'through television and telephony we shall see and hear **(5)** _____ another as perfectly as though we **(6)** _____ face to face, despite intervening distances of thousands of miles.' In 2013, a statue was erected in memory **(7)** _____ Tesla in San Francisco, in the USA. He would **(8)** _____ doubt have been delighted by the fact that visitors can use the free Wi-Fi the statue emits!

Even earlier than Tesla, also in the USA, the writer Mark Twain was another person who appeared to anticipate the internet. In his 1898 short science-fiction story, *From the 'London Times' in 1904*, which was set in his own imminent future, he described a device he called the 'Telectroscope'. This invention was 'connected with the telephonic systems of the world', and it made 'the daily doings of the globe visible to everybody'.

Three decades before Twain, in 1865, the French novelist Jules Verne showed an equally amazing degree of foresight. In his short story *From the Earth to the Moon*, he envisaged a manned spacecraft landing on the surface of the moon. That was more than a hundred years before the first humans landed on the moon in 1969! In Verne's story, the same number of astronauts were on board the spacecraft as in the real Apollo mission, and both fictional and real missions launched from Florida, in the USA. Still more incredibly, Verne's characters in the story experienced a feeling of weightlessness, even though it was not yet known by scientists in 1865 that gravitational forces are different in space.

For an impressive example of even longer-term thinking, take the predictions of the renowned 17th-century Anglo-Irish scientist Robert Boyle. You may have heard of Boyle's law, or the Boyle-Mariotte law, which describes the increase in pressure of a gas as the volume of its container decreases. He is sometimes referred to as 'the father of modern chemistry', but is also admired because he had many other ideas that were far ahead of their time.

In the 1660s, Boyle wrote a 'wish list' in his diary, noting down scientific ideas he thought might come true in the future. Boyle's list started with the hope of increasing life expectancy, which was less than 40 years in England at the time. He suggested that diseases might one day be cured in patients by replacing organs such as the heart or the liver. This anticipated the first successful organ transplant by nearly 300 years! Boyle also expressed the hope that one day scientists would be able to work underwater.

Finally, we must go even further back in time to discover another extraordinarily gifted person who foresaw the future: Leonardo da Vinci. Born in Tuscany (now a region of Italy) in 1452, he is famous for his expertise in an incredible number of fields, including science, architecture, music, art and mathematics. He kept notebooks from the 1480s until he died in 1519, filling them with drawings, diagrams and notes on his research. His notebooks also contain fantastic designs for inventions that would not actually exist for several hundred years.

Although da Vinci's designs were generally ideas rather than very detailed plans, they were remarkable considering the time in which he lived. For instance, da Vinci drew the first ever helicopter-like machine in 1493, 450 years earlier than an actual helicopter would take flight. He also drew a diagram of an early parachute; in 2000, a skydiver called Adrian Nicholas created a parachute using this design, and demonstrated its safety by jumping 3,000 metres from a hot-air balloon. Nicholas said that it provided a less bumpy ride than a modern parachute, despite the fact that the materials Nicholas used were nine times heavier than the ones parachutes are made of today.

GRAMMAR
REVIEW OF FUTURE TENSES

1 Choose the correct options.

1 We need to act quickly if we *'re to recover / will recover* from this crisis.
2 By the end of this week, I *will write / will have written* my first science-fiction story.
3 A new exhibition at the Natural History Museum *will be opening / will have been opening* next month.
4 When I was young, I thought I *will be / was going to be* a professional footballer.
5 Who do you think *will win / will have won* the Nobel Peace Prize this year?
6 By 2032, we *will be sending / will have been sending* satellites into orbit for 75 years.

2 Match the sentences 1–6 in Exercise 1 to the future forms.

Future form	Usage	
future perfect continuous	to focus on the duration of an activity in progress at a time in the future	A
future perfect	to refer to actions or events that will be finished by a time in the future	B
future simple	make predictions and talk about expectations	C
future continuous with *will*	to refer to an activity in progress at a time in the future	D
be to + infinitive	to refer to something that must happen before something else can	E
future in the past	to refer to a future event seen from the past	F

3 Choose the correct options to complete the sentences.

1 By this time next year, I _____ computer science for three years.
  A am studying   B will be studying
  C will have been studying
2 We can't meet in the café at 8 am because it _____ by then.
  A won't have been opening   B won't have opened
  C won't open
3 You should leave now if you _____ the next train.
  A are to catch   B will be catching
  C will catch
4 My sister _____ a year off before going to university, but I talked her out of it.
  A is to take   B will have taken
  C was going to take
5 It is believed that the prime minister _____ an announcement sometime this evening.
  A will have made   B will be making
  C will have been making

4 Rewrite the sentences using the words in brackets.

1 I need to renew my photography club membership next month. (is due to)
  My photography club membership _____.
2 I nearly phoned you, but then you rang the doorbell. (on verge of)
  I was _____.
3 I found the solution just before I gave up. (on point of)
  I was _____.
4 She felt a sneeze coming, so she turned her head away. (was about to)
  She turned _____.

5 Correct the mistakes in the sentences or put a tick by any you think are correct.

1 I never believed that I am going to meet someone like you. _____
2 We don't think we'll be returning in the foreseeable future. _____
3 What do you envisage you'll have been doing this time next year? _____
4 I'll call you as soon as I'll have heard the results of the test. _____
5 He'll have to apply soon if he's to be considered for the job. _____
6 She was on the verge to quit when they offered her a pay rise. _____

6 Complete the blog post with the correct form of the verbs in brackets.

Global action now!

Back in the 19th century, when the Industrial Revolution began, nobody thought it ¹ _____ (have) such a dramatic impact on the world's climate. But the environmental problems we are experiencing now are a direct result of it. If we don't do something soon, we ² _____ (pump) greenhouse gases into the atmosphere for more than 200 years. Action is overdue and essential if we ³ _____ (survive) as a species to the end of this century. It is hoped that by 2030, we ⁴ _____ (cut) down on our use of fossil fuels by at least 70%. It is easy to predict what problems our failure to do so ⁵ _____ (bring). We ⁶ _____ (deal) with the terrible consequences of our lack of action for years to come.

7 Write sentences that are true for you.

1 Think of something that is due to happen soon.
  _____
2 Think of something that was going to happen but didn't.
  _____

VOCABULARY
COMMONLY CONFUSED WORDS

1 Match the words to their definitions.

0 accept	**5** affect	**10** historical
1 except	**6** insure	**11** counsel
2 acquire	**7** assure	**12** council
3 enquire	**8** ensure	
4 effect	**9** historic	

a advise on social or personal problems
b a group of people elected to govern a town or area
c get or buy
d have an influence or cause a change
e protect yourself against risk by buying insurance
f the result of a particular influence
g say yes to an offer
h ask
i apart from
j make sure that something happens
k important in history
l tell someone confidently that something is true so that they do not worry
m relating to past events or people, or to the study of history

0	_g_	2		4		6		8		10		12	
1		3		5		7		9		11			

2 Choose the correct options.

1 You need to contact the local *council / counsel* if you want to complain about parking.
2 Many homes were *effected / affected* by the recent power cuts.
3 Everyone *accept / except* Daniel went on the class history trip.
4 Please *ensure / assure* that all the doors are locked and windows are closed before you leave.
5 Our volleyball team achieved a *historic / historical* victory against our main rivals last week.
6 We *acquired / enquired* about nearby restaurants at the hotel reception.

3 Complete the sentences with words from Exercise 1 in the correct form.

1 He took some medicine, but it didn't have any _____. He still felt ill.
2 Why don't you _____ at the information desk – I'm sure they'll know the answer.
3 It was a _____ moment when the Berlin Wall came down.
4 I _____ you that everything will turn out just fine. Try not to worry about it.
5 The management's poor decisions are _____ my ability to do my job properly.
6 She _____ several new works of art with her winnings.
7 Sorry, I don't know the date of the Russian revolution. My _____ knowledge is very poor.
8 When you buy a new phone, always _____ that you _____ it because they are expensive to replace.
9 I _____ you to write to the _____ about the litter problem in your local park.
10 We _____ all forms of payment here, _____ cheques.

4 Correct the misspelled words.

1 Our science class is seperated into two groups. _____
2 Have you recieved your payment yet? _____
3 I will definately call you in the coming week. _____
4 We were assured that our accomodation would be ready by now. _____
5 Apparently, my car is overdue for a service. _____
6 Do you beleive we will ever colonise Mars? _____
7 I'm not going to accept any unecessary requests. _____
8 It is embarassing how easily we were beaten in that match. _____

✓ PREPARE FOR THE EXAM

Reading and Use of English Part 1

5 For questions 1–8, read the text below and decide which answer (A, B, C or D) best fits each gap.

LIVING IN A SCIENCE-FICTION WORLD

Writers of science fiction have always made predictions about the future. Some of the best sci-fi creators have **(0)** _turned_ out to be remarkably accurate in the long **(1)** _____. Such wonders as submarines, tablet computers and virtual reality all made their first **(2)** _____ in science fiction, decades before they were actually invented.

But what of the predictions that haven't come true? The flying car is one example of something which is unlikely to become a reality in the **(3)** _____ future. Which is just as **(4)** _____. Can you imagine the chaos and destruction?

Another example is the theory known as *the singularity* – the point in time when technology becomes so advanced that it is impossible to control, and computers take over the world. Some people are convinced we are on the **(5)** _____ of this scenario, as envisaged in the classic *Terminator* movies.

But I do not find this idea at all **(6)** _____ – in fact, the best computer scientists **(7)** _____ us that the singularity will never happen. Nevertheless, we do need to **(8)** _____ that the coming years will probably be like living in a science-fiction story.

	A	**B**	**C**	**D**
0	come	found	Ⓒturned	made
1	term	time	age	period
2	arrival	appearance	look	image
3	foreseeable	anticipated	expected	approaching
4	good	fine	sure	well
5	point	verge	start	dawn
6	thinkable	reliable	plausible	definite
7	insure	assure	ensure	inquire
8	accept	take	allow	except

✓ EXAM TIP

Look at the words on both sides of the gap. Sometimes only the correct answer will fit grammatically.

LISTENING

1 How long do you think it takes for a spaceship to travel from Earth to Mars?

A 8 days
B 8 weeks
C 8 months

2 You are going to listen to a talk by a man called Dr Martin Stuart about the research he did for the European Space Agency. Read the first part of the talk and check your answer to Exercise 1.

> Like many a youngster, I dreamed of becoming an astronaut. But I soon came to accept that wasn't a realistic long-term goal – a degree in engineering or science was achievable, but I wasn't suited to military service. Eventually, I decided on psychology, and became a mental-health specialist.
>
> So, you can imagine my excitement when I was invited to take part in a research programme by the European Space Agency in Antarctica. A manned flight to Mars will take around eight months – a long time to be in a confined space with other crew members.

3 Now read question 1 in Exercise 7. What is the correct answer?

....

4 Two other possible (but wrong) answers are mentioned. What are they?

....

5 Now listen to the whole talk. Are the following statements true (*T*) or false (*F*)?

1 Dr Stuart always wanted to be a psychologist. ....

2 The low temperatures are the main source of discomfort for the crew. ....

3 Not all of the crew in Antarctic are involved with the Mars mission. ....

6 Read the questions in Exercise 7. How many can you answer?

Listening Part 2

7 You will hear part of a talk by a man called Dr Martin Stuart, who has just returned from a base in Antarctica where he did research for the European Space Agency. For questions 1–8, complete the sentence with a word or short phrase.

1 Before starting his career, Dr Stuart studied .... at university.

2 Dr Stuart explains that his research focuses on .... and its effects on human behaviour.

3 Dr Stuart says .... is the one thing that cannot be simulated on the Antarctic base.

4 Dr Stuart refers to the base as a .... to show how much the crew rely on it.

5 Dr Stuart uses the words '..........' to describe a characteristic which he believes can be a serious problem.

6 The crew are particularly dependent on the .... to keep their senses stimulated.

7 Dr Stuart feels that not having .... actually benefitted previous Antarctic researchers.

8 Dr Stuart says that the human .... is something that is strongly affected by long hours of darkness.

 **EXAM TIP**

Always read the instructions and the items to get to know the topic. Try to think what kind of information is required in each gap.

8 Answer the questions.

1 Would you like to be an astronaut? Why? / Why not?

....

....

2 What other careers do you think would cause great stress, either physically or mentally?

....

....

READING AND USE OF ENGLISH

1 Choose the correct answers for the questions below.

1 This plane was supposed to take off at 9.45.　　**DUE**
9.45 is the _____ take off.
A time due for this plane to
B time this plane was due to

2 The athlete's performance was negatively affected by her recent injury.　　**HAD**
The athlete's recent injury _____ her performance.
A had a negative effect on
B had a negative affect on

2 Why are the other options incorrect in Exercise 1?

_____
_____
_____

3 Look at question 1 in Exercise 4.

A Which phrasal verb with *over* is another way of saying 'recover from'? _____
B What verb comes after *It*? _____

⊘ PREPARE FOR THE EXAM

Reading and Use of English Part 4

4 For questions 1–6, complete the second sentence so that it has a similar meaning to the first sentence using the word given. Do not change the word given. You must use between three and six words, including the word given.

1 I did not recover from my illness for weeks.　　**ME**
It _____ over my illness.

2 The band appeared on stage just as we were about to leave.　　**POINT**
We were _____ the band appeared on stage.

3 They haven't yet decided on a final date for the festival.　　**STILL**
The final date for the festival _____ air.

4 Mario was the only person they didn't award a scholarship to.　　**EXCEPT**
A scholarship _____ Mario.

5 You should take some driving lessons soon.　　**ABOUT**
It _____ some driving lessons.

6 I have the feeling that something disastrous is going to happen to us very soon.　　**VERGE**
I have the feeling that we _____ disaster.

⊘ EXAM TIP

The key word must always be used and must not be changed in any way.

5 Read the text in Exercise 8, quickly.
Who was Marshal McLuhan?
What did he do?

_____

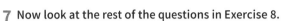

6 Look at the example (0) in Exercise 8. Why are the following options incorrect?

A prediction _____
B predictable _____

7 Now look at the rest of the questions in Exercise 8.

A What parts of speech are required in each?

_____

B Which items require negatives? _____
C Which item requires a plural? _____

⊘ PREPARE FOR THE EXAM

Reading and Use of English Part 3

8 For questions 1–8, read the text below. Use the word given in capitals at the end of some of the lines to form a word that fits in the gap in the same line. There is an example at the beginning (0).

Marshal McLuhan　🔍

Futurists make **(0)** _predictions_ . But did any see the internet coming? There was one man who possessed such remarkable **(1)** _____ . His name was Marshal McLuhan, an author and professor of English from Canada. In his first book, written in 1962, he explained how humanity will experience four **(2)** _____ phases, the last of which he called the 'electronic age'. We are **(3)** _____ still in the electronic age today.　　**PREDICT**　　**FORESEE**　　**HISTORY**　**REPUTE**

In his next book, McLuhan described the world as a **(4)** _____ village – because the effect of international communication was to make the world a smaller place. The accuracy of his vision was **(5)** _____ . He envisaged how information would become instantly accessible to anyone connected to the network, and he anticipated the amazing level of **(6)** _____ that would arise in an online community.　　**GLOBE**　　**CREDIBLE**　　**INTERACT**

He also predicted some of the negative **(7)** _____ of the internet.　　**CHARACTER**

Rampant commercialism and the invasion of privacy, for example, both of which many today view as **(8)** _____ harmful consequences of our technological development.　　**ACCEPT**

⊘ EXAM TIP

This part of the exam tests vocabulary and your ability to form words by adding prefixes (e.g. *happy* → *unhappy*) and suffixes (e.g. *happy* → *happiness*), and by making compound words (e.g. *home* + *work* → *homework*).

4 FOOD FOR THOUGHT

VOCABULARY AND READING
FOOD AND DRINK

1 Match the words and phrases to the definitions.

1 foodie	**6** inedible
2 appetite	**7** leftovers
3 bite to eat	**8** chain
4 culinary	**9** nutritional
5 taste buds	**10** boost

a so bad you can't eat it

b an improvement or an increase

c a number of similar businesses run by the same organisation

d someone who appreciates and is interested in different types of food

e a group of cells that detects whether food is sweet, sour, etc.

f a desire for food

g food that has not been eaten during a meal

h some light food or a small meal

i related to how healthy food is for the body

j related to cooking or kitchens

1	**3**	**5**	**7**	**9**
2	**4**	**6**	**8**	**10**

2 Complete the sentences with the words or phrases from Exercise 1 in the correct form.

1 There's a _____ of restaurants in this city that makes delicious burgers.

2 Are you hungry? Shall we have a _____?

3 It's important to eat food with a high _____ value so you have plenty of energy.

4 I don't want to eat anything – I just don't have much of an _____ at the moment.

5 You've put so much salt in this soup that it's practically _____!

6 My aunt and uncle are real _____ – they always make delicious meals when I go to their house.

7 My _____ skills are improving slowly, especially since I moved into a flat on my own.

8 Fruit and vegetables provide a _____ to your body's immune system.

9 Most of your _____ are on your tongue.

10 I don't need to go shopping or cook today because I have plenty of _____ from the weekend.

3 Complete the sentences so that they are true for you.

1 My favourite leftovers are _____.

2 The most popular restaurant chain in my area is _____.

3 If I want a quick bite to eat, I usually _____.

4 Something I think is inedible is _____.

5 When my health needs a boost, I eat _____.

4 Read quickly what expert A says in the article on the opposite page. Which of the following topics are mentioned?

A people who don't eat meat	**E** where food is grown
B farm animals	**F** environmental issues
C the food people like	**G** water use
D health	**H** transporting food

5 Now read what the other experts say. Do they mention the same topics? Which topic does no one mention?

_____

PREPARE FOR THE EXAM

Reading and Use of English Part 6

6 For questions 1–4, choose from the experts A–D. The experts may be chosen more than once.

Which expert

1 holds a similar opinion to D on whether food ought to be transported over long distances?

2 has a different view from B on the likelihood of large numbers of people giving up meat?

3 has a similar view to A on whether growing some foods that require large amounts of water is justifiable?

4 expresses a different opinion from all the others on the environmental impact of producing meat?

EXAM TIP

There are three different types of question: looking for a similar opinion to the text mentioned in the question, looking for a different opinion to the text mentioned in the question and looking for a text with a different opinion from the three other texts.

7 Match the highlighted words or phrases in the text to the definitions.

1 basic or main _____

2 much _____

3 looking after animals _____

4 an accepted part of the way people live _____

5 animals and birds on a farm _____

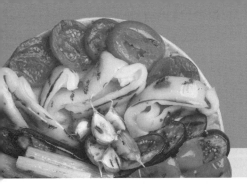

No more MEAT?

Four experts give their opinions

A

Nowadays, few would dispute that the large-scale rearing of beef cattle is bad for the planet. Nevertheless, I fear that the human appetite for meat shows little sign of diminishing. I am aware of the argument that providing people with food of similar nutritional value to meat involves flying vegetables, fruit and grains around the world at huge environmental cost. There is no reason why this should be inevitable, though, given that so many countries have the potential to farm a wide enough variety of food for their own populations, and this should be encouraged. However, a completely different problem has now arisen because of the tastes of vegetarian and vegan foodies worldwide: there is an increasing demand for plants such as avocadoes and almonds which, despite originating from areas with significant and regular rainfall, are currently widely cultivated in places where this cannot be guaranteed. As a result, lakes and rivers are drained to water them, which arguably is almost as harmful to the ecosystem as producing meat.

B

Critics of vegans and vegetarians like to draw attention to the many 'food miles' clocked up by planes carrying fruit and vegetables over very long distances, simply to satisfy their taste buds. And yet, most non-meat eaters are happy to eat food cultivated in their local area. Many are also conscious of the need to avoid certain alternative protein sources, such as almonds, for example, because despite being known to be particularly 'thirsty' crops, these are frequently produced in extremely dry climates. This means using scarce water resources for crops rather than for animals and humans. Moreover, critics of vegetarians should not ignore or gloss over the immense ecological harm caused by the human demand for a regular supply of meat. Sadly, however, they may well be justified in thinking that there is little chance of a serious reduction in this demand globally, at least for the foreseeable future. Some habits take generations to change.

C

We are constantly told that we should stop eating meat because providing what many regard as a staple food invariably involves agricultural practices that accelerate climate change. I am not convinced that this is always the case. Organic meat and dairy production use methods that restore goodness to the soil, and cause minimal harm. In contrast, farming crops like soya on an industrial scale, using pesticides and chemical fertilisers, not only actively destroys the soil, but also pollutes nearby rivers, lakes and ground water. Furthermore, too many vegetarians and vegans seem to think it is perfectly acceptable to eat food that has travelled halfway across the world before it ends up on their plate. This is, unfortunately, often the only way to provide them with the dishes they enjoy. I can only hope that this comes to be recognised as the huge problem it undoubtedly is.

D

Keeping cows, sheep and other livestock is known to cause methane gas emissions that have a negative effect on Earth's atmosphere. The solution, however, should not be to harvest fruit, grain and vegetables in one part of the planet, only to then send them to another continent to be cooked and eaten. All too frequently, sadly, this is exactly what happens. On a more positive note, although there are still those who claim that vegetarian and vegan food is virtually inedible, the increasing number of vegetarian and vegan restaurant chains suggest that many disagree. I believe that this trend is here to stay, and in the not too distant future, vegetarianism and veganism will be the norm. There has been a lot of publicity about the amount of water required to grow some foods, but improvements in agricultural technology and more efficient irrigation techniques mean this problem is essentially solved.

GRAMMAR
INFINITIVES AND GERUNDS

1 Write *to* in the gap where necessary.

1 Luckily, we managed _____ find a restaurant that served vegan food.
2 Have you ever seen Marcus _____ finish an entire meal?
3 Is it true that _____ succeed as a great chef requires both talent and hard work?
4 Tonight, I will attempt _____ cook a meal using last night's leftovers.
5 We used to love watching our mother _____ prepare dinner every evening.
6 Leave the beans in water overnight _____ reduce cooking time.
7 I am thrilled _____ announce the opening of a new Turkish restaurant on Moor Street.
8 We left the restaurant when we heard the chef _____ sneeze in the kitchen.
9 _____ become a top-class chef was her ambition from an early age.
10 I left a generous tip _____ show how happy I was with the food and the service.

2 Choose the correct options. Sometimes two are possible.

1 Maybe you should consider *consume / to consume / consuming* more calories if you want to get stronger.
2 I don't claim *know / to know / knowing* much about Italian food, but I love it.
3 Caroline is very keen for you *try / to try / trying* her new paella recipe.
4 *Become / To become / Becoming* famous is not something he aspires to.
5 I was so hungry that the people downstairs could hear my stomach *rumble / to rumble / rumbling*.
6 Guests are required *dress / to dress / dressing* smartly for this evening's dinner.
7 We all saw the waiter *drop / to drop / dropping* the tray full of glasses.
8 As we drove past the square, we saw someone *set up / to set up / setting up* a new pop-up restaurant.
9 Would anyone object to me *order / to order / ordering* soup instead of a dessert?
10 I'm looking forward to the opportunity *sample / to sample / sampling* the local delicacies while I'm here.

3 Complete the blog post with the gerund or infinitive form (with or without *to*) of the verb in brackets.

0 *Switching* (switch) from meat-eating to a vegetarian diet is not something people do lightly. I considered ¹_____ (make) the change for years before I finally took the decision ²_____ (do) it. Although I still live at home with my parents, I now cook my own food because my mother objected to ³_____ (prepare) a separate meal every day, just for me. I heard one vegetarian friend ⁴_____ (say) that he just eats whatever the rest of the family is eating, except for the meat part. But I would advise against ⁵_____ (do) that because you'll miss out on important nutrients. The main reason I gave up meat was ⁶_____ (help) combat climate change. Apparently, animal farming is responsible for ⁷_____ (produce) 13% of all greenhouse gases, and it makes me anxious ⁸_____ (think) of the future consequences of that.

4 Complete the sentences with the gerund or infinitive form (with or without *to*) of the words in the box.

| advise | boost | break | cook | heat | open |
| order | send | use | | | |

1 The restaurant manager is eager _____ sales with local advertising.
2 _____ even is the best we can hope for in the first few weeks of business.
3 We made the decision _____ a pop-up restaurant in the town square.
4 Would anyone object to me _____ my fingers to eat this pizza?
5 She switched on the oven _____ up the previous evening's leftovers.
6 I have never attempted _____ paella because it looks so complicated.
7 My father warned us against _____ a dish back to a restaurant kitchen.
8 I just heard the waiter _____ a customer not _____ the dish of the day.

👁 5 Correct the mistakes in the sentences or put a tick by any you think are correct.

1 I recommend to add a little more salt to this dish.
2 Guests are permitted smoke in the garden.
3 May I take this opportunity thanking you for a delicious meal.
4 Is there any possibility of meeting the chef when the dinner is over?
5 I have never seen Steven to cook anything in my life.
6 He claims not to know anything about the culinary arts.

6 Complete the sentences so that they are true for you. Use a gerund or infinitive and any other words you need.

1 I have never seen my best friend _____ .
2 The main reason I study is _____ .
3 _____ is not something I ever want to do.
4 If I ever have the opportunity _____ , I will do it.
5 I have never approved of _____ .
6 When I was little, my parents didn't allow me _____ .

FOOD IDIOMS AND EXPRESSIONS

1 Match the halves of the food idioms.

1	have your	plate
2	food for	beans
3	take it with a	cake and eat it
4	not my	pinch of salt
5	spill the	every pie
6	have a lot on your	thought
7	have a finger in	chips
8	cheap as	cup of tea

1 ....
2 ....
3 ....
4 ....
5 ....
6 ....
7 ....
8 ....

2 Respond to each of these situations using a food idiom from Exercise 1.

1 Your friend went on a date last night, and you want them to tell you what happened.
You say: 'Come on, ...!'

2 Somebody tells you something they heard, which you suspect is not true.
You say: 'I'd ....,'

3 A friend wants to save money, but also wants to go out every night.
You say: '..,'

4 Somebody gives you some information which makes you reconsider your situation.
You say: 'Thank you, that ....,'

5 You see an advert in the newspaper saying 'Motorcycle for sale – only £100'.
You say: '..,'

6 You hear about a businessperson who invests in technology, publishing, manufacturing and leisure.
You say: 'She ....,'

7 Somebody invites you to see an opera, but you have never liked opera.
You say: 'No, thanks. ....,'

8 Your friend asks for help, but you have too many things to do at the moment.
You say: 'Sorry, ...,'

WORD FORMATION: SUFFIXES

3 Make words with the suffixes in the box.

> -al   -ally   -ate   -en   -ence   -ily   -ion   -ive

1 communicate (v) .... (adj)
2 exist (v) .... (n)
3 ready (adj) .... (adv)
4 length (n) .... (v)
5 collect (v) .... (n)
6 celebration (n) .... (v)
7 accident (n) .... (adv)
8 benefit (v) .... (adj)

4 Complete the sentences with the words in brackets in the correct form.

1 My friend .... agreed to help me cook dinner. (happy)
2 We had a meal after my brother's .... ceremony. (graduate)
3 We didn't arrange to meet – it was a complete .... (coincide)
4 The teacher doesn't .... bad behaviour in class. (tolerance)
5 These photos are purely .... – they add nothing to the story. (decorate)
6 Our TV switches itself off .... after three hours. (automatic)
7 Leave the bananas to .... for a few days before eating them. (soft)
8 These ready meals are produced on an .... scale. (industry)

 PREPARE FOR THE EXAM

Reading and Use of English Part 3

5 Read the text below. Use the word given in capitals at the end of some of the lines to form a word that fits in the gap in the same line. There is an example at the beginning (0).

Food for thought

If you are preparing for an important exam, or embarking on some other **(0)** _intellectually_ demanding activity, it   **INTELLECT**
might be worth your while paying attention to your diet. Eating **(1)** .... is   **HEALTH**
always good advice, of course, but there is a certain amount of **(2)** .... to   **EVIDENT**
suggest that some types of food might actually **(3)** .... your brain to   **ABLE**
function more efficiently.

Wholegrains, for example. They may be rather **(4)** .... on their own,   **APPETITE**
but wholegrain flour baked into bread or made into pasta is perfectly edible, and some scientists are convinced that it can help with concentration and focus. Additionally, the **(5)** .... of blueberries is said   **CONSUME**
to boost short-term memory – as long as you remember to eat them!

Indeed, the list of foods which are claimed to be **(6)** .... to the brain   **BENEFIT**
is quite long. However, it should be noted that scientific research in this area is still in its **(7)** ...., and can best be   **INFANT**
described as **(8)** .... So, take   **CONCLUDE**
it all with a pinch of salt.

✓ **EXAM TIP**

Look at each gap in context and decide which kind of word is required – noun, verb, adjective or adverb.

WRITING
AN ESSAY

>> SEE *PREPARE TO WRITE* BOX, STUDENT'S BOOK PAGE 33

1 Do you think that the following are a good idea?
Why? / Why not? Make notes.

1 eating meals at regular times

_____

2 eating with other people

_____

3 turning your phone off during meals

_____

4 not watching TV while you eat

_____

2 In your opinion, which of the ideas in Exercise 1 has
the most positive impact on people's lives?

_____

3 Read the task. Are any of the opinions expressed in the
discussion similar to yours?

Your class has listened to a discussion about eating
habits which improve people's well-being. You have
made the notes below.

**Eating habits which can improve people's
well-being:**
• eating at regular times
• sharing meals with other people
• turning off TV, phones, etc. while eating

Some opinions expressed in the discussion:
'It's great to eat whenever you feel like it!'
'Eating together brings families closer.'
'Mealtimes are a chance to have a break
from the world.'

Write an essay discussing **two** of the eating habits in
your notes that improve people's well-being. You should
**explain which habit you think is more effective, giving
reasons** to support your opinion.
You may, if you wish, make use of the opinions
expressed in the discussion, but you should use your
own words as far as possible.

4 Put the paragraphs from the sample essay in the
correct order. Ignore the gaps.

1 _____ 2 _____ 3 _____ 4 _____

A There are several reasons why sharing
meals with other people is beneficial.
(1) _____, humans are social
animals; throughout our history as a species,
meals have been occasions for bringing
people together. **(2)** _____, in
our busy lives, sitting down at least once a
day with our family provides an opportunity
to catch up and maintain important
relationships. Moreover, **(3)** _____
not everyone lives in a family unit, meeting
friends for meals and sharing food gives
many of us a great deal of pleasure.

B To sum up, it seems to me that
the benefits of the first approach
(4) _____ those of the
second. This is because, since we all
have to eat, mealtimes are a perfect
opportunity to strengthen our social bonds.
(5) _____, this need not mean
following strict rules when it comes to such
things as TVs and phones.

C When and how we consume our food
can have a significant effect on our
well-being. **(6)** _____
two ways of approaching mealtimes
that can improve people's quality of life,
(7) _____, sharing meals with
other people and turning off TVs, phones
and any other potential sources of distraction
while eating.

D My second suggestion for enhancing
people's well-being is to avoid the
distractions of the modern world while
eating. **(8)** _____, if our mealtimes
are sociable occasions, we should focus
on the people who are with us. However,
(9) _____, families who have
the news on in the background while eating
often find it stimulates discussion. And if
one is alone, a mealtime may in fact be
an ideal time to message friends or scroll
through newsfeeds.

5 Complete the sample essay, using one of the options below in each gap. Add capital letters where necessary.

a outweigh
b namely
c secondly
d arguably
e firstly
f in my experience
g nevertheless
h although
i I would like to consider

6 Has the student answered the essay question well?

7 Choose the correct options.

1 This is *presented / exemplified* by the number of people eating breakfast while on their way to work.
2 The *good / main* argument for turning off one's phone at the table is that it is rude not to.
3 I would *like / hope* to end by saying that people are unlikely to change their habits overnight.
4 The *arguments / discussions* I have presented indicate that the best option is probably to ban fast food.
5 I am *convinced / determined* that there are better ways to solve the problem.
6 Another crucial *point / aspect* of the problem is price.
7 *One / The* example of this is cheap junk food.
8 From my *view / perspective*, it is important to encourage good habits in children.
9 One *solution / explanation* to the problem would be to teach people about nutrition at school.

8 In which part of an essay would you use the expressions in sentences 1–9 in Exercise 7?

A introduction of main points _____
B introduction of supporting evidence _1_
C giving opinions _____
D concluding the essay _____

9 Read the question and plan your essay. Which two kinds of food are you going to address? Are you going to use any of the opinions given?

> Your class has watched a panel discussion about whether higher taxes should be imposed on certain kinds of food. You have made the notes below.
>
> **Which kinds of food should have higher taxes:**
> * fast food
> * sweets and chocolate
> * ready meals from supermarkets
>
> > **Some opinions expressed in the discussion:**
> > 'Fast food is addictive and bad for you, so should be more expensive.'
> > 'Everyone should be able to have a treat sometimes.'
> > 'People should be encouraged to cook for themselves.'
>
> Write an essay discussing **two** of the kinds of food in your notes. You should **explain which kind of food should have higher taxes, giving reasons** to support your opinion.
> You may, if you wish, make use of the opinions expressed in the discussion, but you should use your own words as far as possible.

 PREPARE FOR THE EXAM

Writing Part 1

10 Write your essay. Use some of the expressions you have learned. Write 220–260 words.

> **✓ EXAM TIP**
>
> Choose the two points you are going to discuss and plan your essay.

5 ON TREND

VOCABULARY AND READING
CLOTHES AND FASHION

1 Complete the sentences below. The first letter of each word is given.

1 That hat looks great on you! The colour's really f _____ because it's almost the same as your eyes.

2 I can't order those trousers online – they don't s _____ them anywhere.

3 My brother's friends see him as a t _____ – he's often among the first to adopt new fashions.

4 My best friend always looks so e _____ stylish. I'm not like that at all – I have to try quite hard!

5 A lot of people like to f _____ i _____, so they try to dress like everybody else.

6 I'm trying to save money, so it's a been a while since I went on a s _____ s _____.

7 She has e _____ taste – she wears all kinds of different clothes.

8 Sometimes, she wears quite dull and formal clothes, and at other times, she wears things that are very e _____ - c _____.

9 You look very smart in that t _____ suit!

10 Sometimes you can get s _____ at a very reasonable price. It's one way of dressing more cheaply, but there may be small marks on the clothes.

2 Match the definitions to the answers from Exercise 1.

A dress in a similar style to the people around you _____

B someone whose clothes and style are imitated by other people _____

C very attractive or noticeable _____

D making someone look good _____

E including many different styles _____

F without trying _____

G clothes that are cheaper because they are not in perfect condition _____

H keep a supply of a product in a shop _____

I a shopping trip where a lot of things are bought _____

J made to specifically fit someone's body well _____

3 Complete the sentences with the answers from Exercise 1 in the correct form.

1 Don't worry about _____ in by wearing the same kinds of clothes as everyone at your new college.

2 She looks _____ beautiful, but in fact, she spends a lot of time making sure she looks perfect.

3 I'm afraid we don't _____ the coat you want any more, sir.

4 Yellow isn't a _____ colour for everyone – some people look awful in it.

5 My friends went on a _____ last weekend. They have no money left!

6 I suppose my taste in clothes is pretty _____ – I don't stick to one particular style.

4 Read the first three paragraphs of the article on the opposite page, ignoring the gaps. Which of the following could be an alternative title?

A A successful decision
B How I dress to impress
C Time to find new friends

 PREPARE FOR THE EXAM

Reading and Use of English Part 3

5 For questions 1–8, read the text on the opposite page. Use the word given in capitals at the end of some of the lines to form a word that fits in the gap in the same line. There is an example at the beginning (0).

 EXAM TIP

You always have to change the given word.

6 Read the rest of the article and answer the questions below.

In which paragraph (A–F) does the writer say

1 concerns about what to wear can be addressed without having to buy anything? _____

2 she felt freer after becoming aware that others didn't notice her clothes? _____

3 enjoyment need not depend on acquiring something new? _____

4 not buying things inspired her to alter clothes she already owned? _____

5 she found different role models when it came to clothes? _____

6 she feared that she would be criticised? _____

7 some advice should not be followed? _____

8 she used to think that something was too hard for her to do well? _____

9 she carried on buying clothes, but from a different source? _____

10 she realises that an expectation is unrealistic? _____

11 there is a solution that too few people consider? _____

12 the majority of her efforts had the desired result? _____

7 Match the **highlighted** words in the text to the definitions.

1 found something after having to search for it
_____

2 prepare yourself for something (often unpleasant)
_____

3 people who recommend something
_____

4 checks someone or something very carefully
_____

5 bad luck, or a little problem or accident
_____

A year without buying new clothes

I can't remember a new year when I haven't made a **(0)** _resolution_. Get more sleep, eat more fruit, learn a new language, etc. But there's only one promise I've ever **(1)** .... stuck to for longer than a few weeks, and it's possibly the only one that's ever made me feel better about myself – I broke up with fast fashion.

No brand new clothes for a year. No more casual flirtation with one of the most exploitative and **(2)** .... industries on the planet. Goodbye, my friend, who has so often proved **(3)** .... Before you say it, I know: not shopping shouldn't be a **(4)** .... For plenty of people it's normal, through **(5)** .... to afford it or just lack of interest.

Over the years, clothes have been my comfort blanket and **(6)** .... booster. They've been a hobby in my spare time, a **(7)** .... sport and a way to bond with people. I've used clothes to draw attention to myself, and I've used them as camouflage – buying the illusion of grown-up **(8)** .... at a time when my salary was extremely low.

RESOLVE

SUCCEED

WASTE
PROBLEM
HARD
ABLE

CONFIDENT
COMPETE

PROFESSIONAL

A I know I gave them too much time – and money. Once I stopped going on spending sprees, spare cash appeared in my account, and periods of free time began to appear in my week. To be clear, I didn't stop shopping entirely. Charity shops effortlessly filled the gap left by the high street, along with the occasional preowned treasure discovered on the internet. But second-hand shopping is a very different concept – it's the slow-release of energy to fast fashion's sugar rush. While the high street sells the idea that every shopping trip should involve splashing out, charity shops manage your expectations. Going home empty-handed feels less like defeat. You've saved the money, and still had a nice day out.

B I also learned new tricks to get more wear out of my existing wardrobe, like layering – an artform I'd previously believed was beyond people like me. It turns out it's not! You simply take your clothes and . . . put them on top of other clothes to create eye-catching outfits. Slim-fit polo necks under sleeveless tops, shirts under short-sleeved sweaters, jumpers over dresses over jeans, etc. Aside from one mishap with a mustard knitted sleeveless top and a white shirt, I had a surprisingly good success rate.

C As so many business gurus will tell you, restrictions force creativity. And when you limit your shopping options, you find yourself getting inventive with new tools instead. Sometimes superglue, sometimes scissors. My sewing skills had become a bit rusty since I was at school, but after I stopped shopping, I started doing a bit more – I'd make a skirt shorter, change the shape of a neckline, etc. When a desire for some new summer clothes hit last month, I unearthed an ancient pair of trousers, and turned them into a flattering pair of shorts. They weren't exactly the shorts of my dreams, but they were close enough. And I'm old enough to know by now that the shorts of my dreams don't exist.

D Ignore anyone who tells you to get rid of everything you haven't worn in a year. Fashion is cyclical – come on, we know this – and no sooner have you sent an old jacket off to the charity shop than a fashion magazine will suddenly declare it's trending again. 'The most sustainable item is the one you already own,' says Fashion Revolution (the global movement that scrutinises industry practices). It's amazing how often you can solve a contemporary fashion dilemma with something that's already in your wardrobe.

E And if not yours, someone else's. Sharing and borrowing from trendsetting friends is a secret weapon that most of us don't take nearly enough advantage of. Meanwhile, social media took on a new role in my life. I unfollowed every brand and influencer that might have led me to temptation, and let slow-fashion advocates set a new pace on my feed. In a galaxy of eclectic single-wear wardrobes, their willingness to show off the same items again and again felt gently subversive. Following their example, I've become a serial outfit repeater – and proud of it. Nobody has ever said anything.

F In fact, one of the more ego-bruising, but ultimately liberating parts, of the whole process was realising just how little anybody cares what I'm wearing – either at a work meeting or a party. Every time I pulled on the same old outfit, I braced myself for people's disapproval of me for not fitting in because everyone else seemed to change their clothes nearly every day. It never happened. Because, and I really can't stress this enough, people don't care what you wear.

GRAMMAR
REVIEW OF MODALS

1 Choose the correct modal to complete the sentences.

0 I think this blouse ___*might*___ go well with my blue skirt.
A can   **B** might   **C** must

1 You really _____ to cut down on the amount of money you spend on clothes.
A ought   **B** should   **C** could

2 Customers _____ show a valid receipt when returning unwanted items.
A must   **B** can   **C** could

3 In Elizabethan England, nobody _____ wear purple, except the queen.
A should   **B** could   **C** must

4 You _____ bought those jeans while they were in the sale – they're twice the price now!
A might have   **B** ought to   **C** should have

5 I'm not sure where Martha is, but she _____ have gone to the fashion show.
A might   **B** must   **C** can

6 Her outfit is by a famous designer, so it _____ have cost a lot of money.
A can't   **B** must   **C** can

2 Match the modal functions to the sentences 1–6 in Exercise 1.

A obligation _____
B advice _____
C speculation in the present ___*0*___
D permission _____
E speculation in the past _____
F retrospective advice _____

3 Complete the conversations with a modal and the verb in brackets.

0 A: I bought this shirt and it doesn't fit. Can I have my money back?
B: I'm sorry. If you want to return an item, you _*must have*_ a valid receipt. (have)

1 A: These jeans aren't very flattering, are they?
B: Maybe you _____ a slightly more loose-fitting pair. (try)

2 A: Where's Jane? I haven't seen her for hours.
B: I have no idea. She _____ on one of her spending sprees. (be)

3 A: Look, I bought you that dress you said you liked.
B: You _____ that! It's much too expensive! (do)

4 A: I love your baseball cap. It's really eye-catching.
B: You _____ it if you like. I think it'll suit you. (borrow)

5 A: The zip on my trousers is broken, and I don't know how to fix it.
B: Pity. There used to be a tailor on this street who _____ (repair) anything.

6 A: I ordered a pair of jeans from a company in America, but they still haven't arrived.
B: That's strange – they _____ (delay) at customs or something.

EXPRESSIONS WITH MODAL MEANINGS

4 Rewrite the sentences with the word in brackets.

1 These vouchers are not meant to be used to buy non-essential items.
You _____ these vouchers to buy non-essential items. (supposed)

2 No children in the swimming pool after 10 pm.
Children _____ in the swimming pool after 10 pm. (permitted)

3 Unfortunately, we were unable to get a refund for the damaged items.
We _____ to get a refund on the damaged items, unfortunately. (manage)

4 You can only have a refund if the item is undamaged.
If the item is undamaged, _____ a refund. (entitled)

5 Correct the mistakes in the sentences or put a tick by any you think are correct.

1 If only I would have known there was a designer clothes sale on yesterday. _____
2 Try these trousers – they can fit you. _____
3 Everyone is free choosing what activities they want to do tomorrow. _____
4 Students are entitled to a 20% discount on all purchases. _____

✓ PREPARE FOR THE EXAM

Reading and Use of English Part 2

6 For questions 1–8, read the text below and think of the word which best fits each gap. Use only one word in each gap. There is an example at the beginning (0).

Fashion on a budget

I get a lot of emails from readers asking how they **(0)** ___*can*___ dress fashionably on a budget. Firstly, I would like to emphasise that if you want to dress well, you are not obliged **(1)** _____ splash out on designer clothes. It is perfectly possible to look effortlessly stylish **(2)** _____ going on a crazy spending spree. You just have to know where to look.

For me, charity shops are the places to go. **(3)** _____ as *thrift stores* in the USA, there is **(4)** _____ better source for cut-price, second-hand clothes. You might even find the hottest designer labels at ridiculous prices, but that **(5)** _____ not to be your main reason for shopping there. You are looking for **(6)** _____ unique that looks good on you – and you'll probably find it. I'm frequently amazed **(7)** _____ the eclectic range of styles you can find in these places, and I think you will **(8)** _____ too.

✓ EXAM TIP

Look at each gap in context and decide which kind of word is required – noun, verb, adjective or adverb.

VOCABULARY
COMPOUND ADJECTIVES AND NOUNS

1 Complete the sentences with the words in the box.

> fashioned fitting (x2) heeled lasting
> sleeved (x2) wearing

1 You'll need some hard-_____ boots if you're going to work on a building site.
2 I prefer to wear loose-_____ clothes, as they allow more freedom of movement.
3 It's possible to find some lovely old-_____ clothes in charity shops.
4 Not everyone believes that T-shirts must be short-_____, but I do.
5 It can be quite tricky to walk in high-_____ shoes if you haven't done it before.
6 With a dinner suit, it is always necessary to wear a long-_____ shirt.
7 Cyclists wear tight-_____ Lycra clothing because it helps them ride faster.
8 This deodorant has a very long-_____ effect, so you only have to use it once per day.

2 Complete the sentences with compound adjectives from Exercise 1.

1 My grandmother always wore _____ clothes, which wouldn't have looked so good on a younger person.
2 This corset is so _____ that I can't even breathe properly.
3 I always wear a _____ top to protect my arms when I go out in the sun.
4 _____ shoes look good, but they are impractical to wear on the beach.
5 This perfume smells lovely, but unfortunately it isn't very _____ – it wears off after about an hour!
6 We are so confident that our sun hat is the most _____ you have ever owned that it carries a lifetime guarantee.
7 My brother, the bodybuilder, always wears _____ shirts to show off his biceps.
8 I need to wear a belt with these trousers because they're a bit _____ around the waist.

3 Match the words to make compound nouns.

1 bow	gown
2 rain	trunks
3 wet	dress
4 dinner	tie
5 dressing	coat
6 evening	suit
7 swimming	shirt
8 sweat	jacket

1 _____	5 _____
2 _____	6 _____
3 _____	7 _____
4 _____	8 _____

4 Match the descriptions to the compound nouns in Exercise 3.

1 You would wear these to the beach. _____
2 A person, usually a woman, might wear this on a formal occasion. _____
3 You would wear this in wet weather. _____
4 Wear this for protection and warmth when in the sea. _____
5 You might wear this round your shirt collar on a formal occasion. _____
6 A person might wear this at home over their pyjamas. _____
7 You wear this over your shirt as part of a formal suit. _____
8 You would usually wear this informal item of clothing over a T-shirt. _____

5 Answer the questions so that they are true for you.

1 In what situation might you wear a dinner jacket? _____
2 When might you wear a wetsuit? What would you be doing? _____
3 Think of two situations in which someone might wear a bow tie. _____
4 When do you or would you wear a dressing gown? _____
5 Which countries do you think sell the most raincoats? _____
6 How many sweatshirts do you own? When do you wear them? _____

LISTENING

1 You are going to listen to an interview with a fashion photographer and a fashion editor. Which job would you prefer to do? Why?

2 Read question 1 in Exercise 6. Underline the key verb in the question.

3 Write some other words which have the same meaning as the correct answer for Exercise 2.

4 Listen to the extract and answer question 1 in Exercise 6.

5 Now look at the extract and underline the part(s) which reveal the answer. **Highlight** the sections which refer to the wrong options in the question.

> I come from quite an arty family. My mother's a portrait artist, and my dad's a sculptor. They were very productive. And they were both keen for me to develop my creativity. I ended up taking a slightly different path. I was enchanted by stories – both reading and, eventually, writing them. I loved literature of any kind – that's what really drove me in this direction. Add to that the fact that my mother was really into fashion, and that no doubt influenced me a little bit, too – though I was never as obsessed as she was. At least not until I started writing professionally about it. Now she comes to me for fashion advice!

Listening Part 3

6 You'll hear an interview in which a fashion editor called Tina Green and a fashion photographer called Gary Mansfield are talking about their jobs. For questions 1–6, choose the answer (A, B, C or D) which best fits according to what you hear.

1 What motivated Tina to become a fashion editor?
   A a passion for the written word
   B an encouraging relative
   C a fascination for clothing
   D a strong creative impulse

2 What does Gary most enjoy about fashion photography?
   A the opportunity to work with others
   B the artistic possibilities it offers
   C the feeling of independence
   D the variety of locations

3 They agree that the biggest problem with the fashion industry is that it
   A contributes to environmental problems.
   B encourages a materialistic world view.
   C creates unrealistic goals.
   D neglects diversity.

4 How does Tina feel about her job as fashion editor?
   A annoyed that many people misunderstand it
   B happy about the opportunities it presents
   C discouraged by the amount of work involved
   D confident that she can rise to any challenge

5 What advice does Gary give to an aspiring fashion photographer?
   A Learn some business skills.
   B Make contacts in the business.
   C Obtain the relevant qualifications.
   D Take as many photos as possible.

6 When Gary talks about his future career, he reveals his
   A desire to form his own company.
   B satisfaction with his current position.
   C determination to move on to something new.
   D impatience with his lack of creative progress.

EXAM TIP

The questions focus on the opinions, attitudes and feelings of the speakers. There is usually a question about agreement or disagreement between the speakers, too.

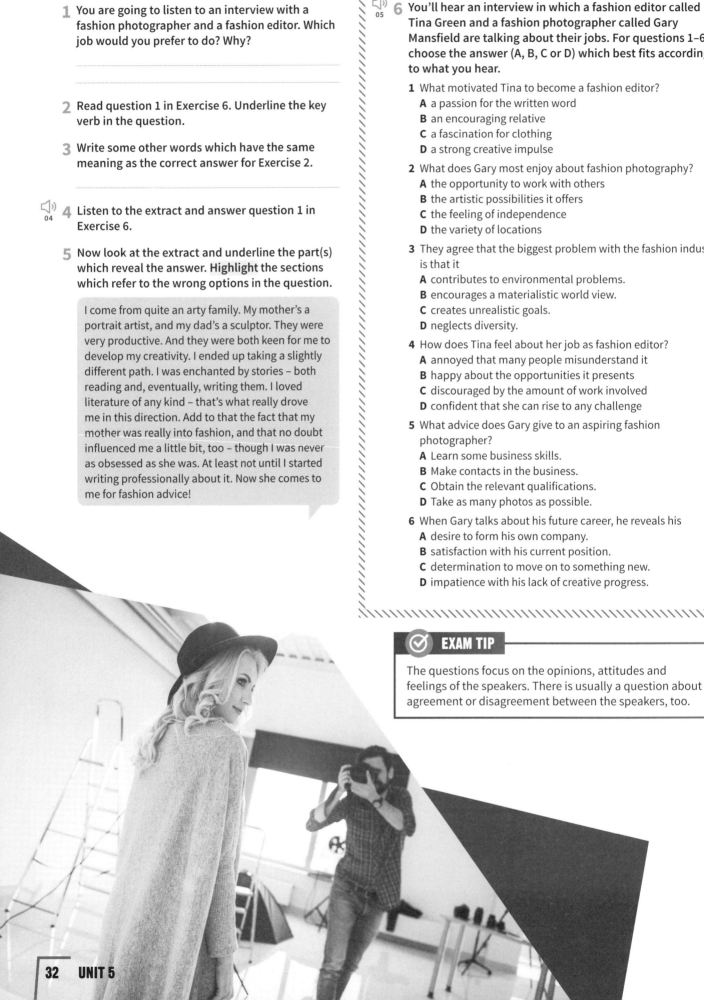

READING AND USE OF ENGLISH

1 Choose the correct answers.

1 Resigning is an option that is always open to you.   **FREE**
You _____ at any time.
A are free resigning
B can freely resign
C are free to resign

2 Speaking to your sister like that was very wrong.   **SHOULD**
You _____ to your sister like that.
A should not have spoken
B should speak more respectfully
C really should not be speaking so rudely

2 Why would the other options in Exercise 1 be incorrect in Reading and Use of English Part 4?

_____

_____

PREPARE FOR THE EXAM

Reading and Use of English Part 4

3 For questions 1–6, complete the second sentence so that it has similar meaning to the first sentence, using the word given. Do not change the word given. You must use between three and six words, including the word given.

1 There is a great deal to think about in this fascinating book.   **FOOD**
This fascinating book will give you

_____ .

2 She bought an expensive new car with her prize money.   **SPLASH**
She used her prize money
_____ an expensive new car.

3 My brother enjoys science-fiction films, but I don't.   **CUP**
Science-fiction films _____ ,
but my brother enjoys them.

4 Cancelling your subscription is something you can do at any time.   **FREE**
You _____ your subscription at any time.

5 It is possible that she received her invitation after the event.   **HAVE**
She _____ her invitation until after the event.

6 It was a mistake for Mark to lend that money to my brother.   **OUGHT**
Mark _____ that money to my brother.

EXAM TIP

Remember not to use more than six words. Contractions such as *it's* or *can't* count as two words.

4 Complete the sentences with the words in the box in the correct form. There are two words you don't need.

> based   define   derive   mention   name   refer

1 In the dictionary, the word 'beauty' is _____ as 'the quality of being beautiful'.
2 Tania was _____ as the 'most improved student' in the year.
3 Somebody _____ that you might be interested in joining the photography club.
4 Muhammad Ali is frequently _____ to as the greatest boxer of all time.

5 Now complete gap 7 in Exercise 6.

 PREPARE FOR THE EXAM

Reading and Use of English Part 1

6 For questions 1–8, read the text below and decide which answer (A, B, C or D) best fits each gap. There is an example at the beginning (0).

The HALO Effect

When we meet someone for the first time, according to psychologists, we tend to **(0)** *make* some very quick judgements about them **(1)** _____ on their physical attractiveness. It only takes seven seconds to form a negative opinion. This is why it is so easy to get off on the wrong **(2)** _____ with someone. After that, whatever they do just seems to **(3)** _____ you up the wrong way. However, if they are attractive, we will **(4)** _____ all sorts of qualities to them, such as intelligence, honesty and good morals. This psychological **(5)** _____ is known as the *halo effect* – one of the many cognitive traps which the human brain can fall into. Unfortunately, avoiding such traps is easier **(6)** _____ than done.

Film stars and models all benefit from the halo effect, which psychologists sometimes **(7)** _____ to as 'the physical attractiveness stereotype.' But you do not have to be rich and famous. Research has shown that good-looking food servers in restaurants earn much more money per year in tips than their less attractive colleagues, **(8)** _____ of the quality of the service.

0 A do	**(B)** make	**C** state	**D** declare
1 A built	**B** set	**C** based	**D** derived
2 A leg	**B** shoe	**C** step	**D** foot
3 A push	**B** rub	**C** wipe	**D** scratch
4 A assert	**B** attribute	**C** denote	**D** apply
5 A occurrence	**B** situation	**C** phenomenon	**D** event
6 A told	**B** shown	**C** described	**D** said
7 A mention	**B** name	**C** refer	**D** define
8 A regardless	**B** irrelevant	**C** nevertheless	**D** despite

EXAM TIP

Think carefully about the meanings of all the words in the options.

6 THE GREAT ESCAPE

VOCABULARY AND READING
TRAVEL AND TOURISM

1 Choose the correct options.

1 I prefer to go to *long-haul / lesser-known / solo* places because they're usually quieter than more popular destinations.

2 I might try to find a *getaway / indigenous / seasonal* job abroad this summer.

3 You should avoid coming to my home town in August. It's a real *package / tourist / weekend* trap.

4 This area is famous for its *unspoilt / getaway / long-haul* beaches.

5 Can we afford a *package / city / weekend* away?

6 If you choose a *package / solo / getaway* tour, your food and accommodation will be included.

7 I work as a tourist guide and educate visitors about our local *once-in-a-lifetime / indigenous / seasonal* culture.

8 Is being a *solo / once-in-a-lifetime / tourist* traveller sometimes lonely?

9 We usually spend our weekends walking in the countryside, so let's do something completely different and go on a *city / getaway / tourist* break.

10 Some people enjoy *once-in-a-lifetime / indigenous / long-haul* travel, and don't mind spending many hours on a plane.

11 That travel agent specialises in relatively cheap, last-minute *cultures / getaways / travellers*.

12 This was going to be a *package / tourist / once-in-a-lifetime* holiday – they had planned it for months.

2 Complete the sentences with the adjective-noun combinations from Exercise 1.

0 This is a really interesting book about the *indigenous culture* of the place we're going to next month.

1 I think that _____ is bad for the planet, and unnecessary – there's no need to fly so far to go on holiday.

2 Let's go on a _____ so we don't have to book our own hotel and figure out what we're going to do for two weeks.

3 He's very independent, and has had some amazing experiences as a _____ .

4 We went to some _____ up in the mountains. They weren't even in our guide book!

5 I think this will be a _____ – we'll remember it for ever!

6 Do you think I'll be able to get a _____ in a hotel? I need to earn a bit of money to help with my studies.

7 This coast has many _____ . The sand is beautiful, and they haven't been touched by tourists yet.

8 The most famous place in the area is a horrible _____ – so many people go there, you can't move.

3 Read the first paragraph of the article on the opposite page. Where were the people staying?

A on a container ship

B in a lake in Cornwall, England

C in a little house made out of a shipping container

4 Read the rest of the article, ignoring the gaps, and answer the questions.

1 How many people were on the holiday?

_____

2 Who owned the place where they were staying?

_____

3 Were they able to make their own meals?

_____

4 Where did they do some exciting and unusual things?

_____

 PREPARE FOR THE EXAM

Reading and Use of English Part 7

5 You are going to read an extract from an article about an interesting holiday. Six paragraphs have been removed from the extract. Choose from the paragraphs A–G the one which fits each gap (1–6). There is one extra paragraph which you do not need to use.

 EXAM TIP

If there are reference words in the text and options, such as *this* or *that*, make sure you find the words that they refer to.

6 Match the highlighted words or phrases in the text to the definitions.

1 free _____

2 with good-quality appliances _____

3 hanging (often from a rope) _____

4 brief view or sight _____

5 without electricity from the public supply system _____

Staying in a shipping container
in Cornwall

It's a terrible thing to realise you have no imagination. When I sailed across the Atlantic on a container ship – a once-in-a-lifetime experience – at no point on the voyage did I think, 'one of those containers would make a great place to stay.' Yet here we were, a friend and I, having a weekend away and planning what to cook for dinner while sitting in what may be the country's most comfortable shipping container, next to a lake on Cornwall's Bodmin Moor, in the southwest of England.

1

'We're well over 300 metres above sea level,' said Rupert, the owner, who grew up on this land. He and his wife Frances were inspired to open this perfect place for a getaway by years of camping here themselves, in a much more basic container. The altitude was something which we had experienced for ourselves, having cycled up from the nearest station, about 8 kilometres away. Indeed, that had proved too much for my companion's bike, but Rupert had kindly raced over and succeeded in fixing it.

2

Rupert told us that a boatbuilder friend of his had fitted the container out, and with its smart wooden exterior and imaginatively used space inside, it had a nautical feel. The well-equipped kitchen had a full-sized gas cooker. A small dining table was covered with complimentary food and had a lovely view of the sun burning the mist off the lake, revealing lots of birds swooping joyfully about. A bathroom was hidden away around the back, with a shower.

3

But the best thing about the container was that the side facing the lake was almost all window. It not only made us feel a part of the scenery, but also meant we could enjoy the sight of dozens of wild moorland ponies walking down for a drink.

4

By day, keen to explore the moor, we took a picnic and climbed various hills, before stopping at a traditional inn for a drink in the village of Blisland. We were served by a landlady who welcomed us extremely kindly.

5

The next morning, we headed out to a nearby activity centre called Adrenalin Quarry. We happily zipwired, learned how to throw axes (a useful skill if the world ever gets taken over by zombies) and were thrown to our certain deaths on a giant swing – or at least that's what you might imagine if you saw my expression as we were launched into the abyss below.

6

And that's a state of affairs that looks set to last. It's unlikely ever to become a tourist trap, full of people on city breaks. 'We'll only ever have one container down here,' Rupert told us. 'You don't want people staring at you from across the water.'

A On arriving back after our hike, we made the most of the late afternoon sun by rowing out onto the lake. My companion dived off the boat – a brave move given that the 25 metres of water underneath us was still far from warm in late spring. I would have joined her, of course, but someone had to row the boat back.

B As we continued, the road and civilisation disappeared. Then, a long track took us to the lake through the former Glynn Valley China Clay Factory, and we had our first glimpse of the cabin ahead of us.

C That craziness was a total contrast to the rest of our day, during which we were largely content simply to sit and watch the light changing on the lake and listen to the birdsong, delighting in the wonderful sense of isolation.

D Nevertheless, it's one of those lesser-known places favoured by solo travellers because of its unspoilt beaches, and seasonal jobs are often available. That wasn't why we were staying in the container, however. Our aim was to discover the indigenous culture.

E Behind them, above the fields, we could see the distant peak of Brown Willy, which, at 420 metres, is the highest point in the county. The area was soon to be given Dark Sky Park status because of the almost total lack of artificial light, and at night we were treated to thousands of stars.

F We'd just arrived, and were impressed by the location. In a beautiful, sheltered spot, it even has its own little private range of hills nearby for guests to climb. These were created by big piles of stone and soil, dug out when clay used to be mined in the area. Nature has spent over 70 years covering them with grass and plants.

G Since we were entirely off-grid, the fact that hot water came out of this was a welcome bonus in the mornings. Solar panels recharged those gadgets we should have left at home and powered a large number of bright LED lights. Only our fridge was really basic – it consisted of a shopping basket suspended in the shallow waters at the edge of the lake, and did its job admirably.

GRAMMAR
MODIFYING COMPARATIVE AND SUPERLATIVE ADJECTIVES

1 Choose the correct options.

1 Commuting by bike is *considerably / among* more eco-friendly than commuting by car.

2 We always get an apartment near the sea so that we can spend the longest time *by far / possible* on the beach every day.

3 I liked Chicago, but it wasn't *such / as* an impressive city as New York.

4 The once-in-a-lifetime trip to Nepal was *one of / somewhat* the most profound experiences of my life.

5 It's much cheaper *renting / to rent* a holiday flat for a week than to stay in a hotel.

6 We complained about the condition of our room, but the new room they gave us wasn't *any / even* better.

7 Parts of the north of Scotland have *such / as* beautiful a landscape as anywhere in the world.

2 Match the grammar rules below to the sentences 1–7 in Exercise 1.

A Modifiers such as *even*, *a great deal*, *considerably*, *substantially* and *somewhat* can be used before comparative adjectives. _____

B Modifiers such as *by far*, *easily*, *one of* and *among* can be used before superlative adjectives. _____

C *No* or *not any* can form the negative before a comparative adjective. _____

D We can use a postmodifier (e.g. *possible*, *ever*, *by far*) to make the superlative stronger, in the structure superlative + postmodifier, or superlative + noun + postmodifier. _____

E A comparative adjective can be followed by *to* infinitive + *than* + *to* infinitive. _____

F We can make comparisons using structures with *as*: *(not) as* + adjective + *a/an* + noun + *as* _____

G We can make comparisons using structures with *such*: *not such* + *a/an* + adjective + noun + *as* _____

3 Rewrite the sentences using the comparative or superlative structure from Exercise 2 in brackets.

0 Travelling by train is more economical than flying. (E)
It *is more economical to travel by train than to fly.*

1 You're a more skilful player than I am. (G)
I'm not _____.

2 We have never had such a great weekend getaway. (D)
It was our _____.

3 Paris is a much more expensive city than Berlin. (A)
Berlin is _____.

4 The first tour was boring, and the second tour was equally boring. (C)
The second tour _____.

5 Lisbon is as beautiful a city as any I have ever visited. (B)
Lisbon is _____.

6 Simon is equally enthusiastic about travelling as his sister. (F)
Simon's sister is _____.

4 Put a tick next to the correct sentence in each pair. Sometimes both are correct.

0 A: I've never been boreder than when I got stranded at the airport for two days. _____
B: I've never been more bored that when I got stranded at the airport for two days. ✓

1 A: That joke isn't any funnier than the first time you told it. _____
B: That joke isn't any more funny than the first time you told it. _____

2 A: You think I care, but you couldn't be wronger. _____
B: You think I care, but you couldn't be more wrong. _____

3 A: I thought she'd have been gratefuller for the help I gave her. _____
B: I thought she'd have been more grateful for the help I gave her. _____

4 A: Just download the app and place your order – it couldn't be simpler. _____
B: Just download the app and place your order – it couldn't be more simple. _____

5 A: The film was much more moving than I expected. _____
B: The film was much movinger than I expected. _____

6 A: I'd say the sky looks greyer than blue today. _____
B: I'd say the sky looks more grey than blue today. _____

👁 5 Correct the mistakes in the sentences or put a tick by any you think are correct.

1 Springtime is far the best season to visit my country.
_____

2 I have never known such gentle animal as my neighbour's dog. _____

3 Her seat on the return journey was no more comfortable than the one she had on the way out. _____

4 Your hair looks more browner than blond at the moment.
_____

5 Our previous teacher was considerably cleverer than the current one. _____

6 Thankfully, it wasn't such as expensive hotel as the one we stayed in last time. _____

6 Complete the blog post using one word in each gap.

Monsoon holiday ≡ 🔍

I'm writing this post from my hotel room. This was supposed to be the best holiday [1] _____, but I have never been [2] _____ bored than I am right now. Coming to the Maldives during the monsoon season was not [3] _____ a brilliant idea as I thought it was. Sure, the tickets were a [4] _____ deal cheaper than for any other time of the year. Now I know why – it's been raining since I arrived.

The hotel itself is nice, which is a relief because it's by [5] _____ the most expensive hotel I've ever stayed in! The food here is fine, but, to be honest, no [6] _____ than what I can get for half the price in my home town.

The hotel manager says the weather will improve tomorrow, and I hope he's right. It would have been much wiser of me to stay at home [7] _____ to spend all that money coming here to sit in a hotel room. This was not [8] _____ of my best decisions!

VOCABULARY
ADVERBS AND ADJECTIVES

1 Put the adjectives in the correct column.

> excited   fascinating   fortunate   fresh
> hazardous   magnificent   remote   stunning
> terrifying   tiny   tranquil   unspoilt

gradable	ungradable

2 Choose the correct options.

1 The mountains of Tibet looked *extremely / utterly* magnificent in the light of the setting sun.

2 It was a *fairly / completely* hazardous journey to the top, but we survived.

3 Our professor was *a bit / absolutely* furious when he discovered that none of us had read his book.

4 In spite of the occasional electricity pylon, the countryside was *reasonably / a bit* unspoilt.

5 You will find it *extremely / completely* impossible to cross the border without the necessary documents.

6 The feeling you get when you first see the Grand Canyon is *very / totally* unique.

3 Does the adverb *quite* make the adjective S (stronger) or W (weaker)?

1 My friend didn't enjoy the flight, but I found it **quite exciting**. _____

2 Her performance on stage that night was **quite magnificent**. _____

3 Unfortunately, it was **quite impossible** to get tickets for the performance. _____

4 It's **quite interesting** to see your home town from a height of 10,000 metres. _____

5 The online reviews for this package holiday were **quite negative**, but we enjoyed ourselves. _____

6 I was **quite astounded** to receive a bill from your magazine, two years after I cancelled my subscription. _____

4 Complete the rules with *strengthens* or *weakens*.

1 *quite* + gradable adjective _____ the adjective.

2 *quite* + ungradable adjective _____ the adjective.

5 Choose the correct adverbs to complete the sentences.

1 Her style is _____ unique. No one else dresses like her.
A totally   **B** perfectly   **C** deeply

2 I was _____ proud of myself when I finished the race. I never thought I could do it.
A fully   **B** genuinely   **C** highly

3 That animal is _____ unusual. Look at its nose.
A fully   **B** deeply   **C** highly

4 I am _____ aware that the journey will be quite hazardous.
A actively   **B** fully   **C** utterly

5 The whole country remains _____ committed to environmental sustainability.
A perfectly   **B** a bit   **C** deeply

Reading and Use of English Part 1

6 Read the text below and decide which answer (A, B, C or D) best fits each gap.

JOBS:
TOUR LEADER

Working as a tour leader is an increasingly **(0)** *popular* option, especially among young graduates looking for a fun job before embarking on a more serious career path. Some see it as getting paid to go on holiday.

But do not be deceived. Tour leading for a travel company is very much a proper job, involving a great **(1)** _____ of hard work. Indeed, it can lead to a life-long career in an industry full of **(2)** _____ committed professionals.

A tour leader's hours are long. As you are responsible for your clients, it is perfectly **(3)** _____ to be on call 24/7. **(4)** _____ you are leading a group of walkers in the Pyrenees or doing a cultural tour of European cities, you can be **(5)** _____ certain something will go wrong at some **(6)** _____ – and you will have to deal with it.

(7) _____ if you decide not to stay in the business, tour leading is excellent training for a future career in that it is likely to significantly **(8)** _____ your people-handling and problem-solving skills.

0 **A** favourite	**B** popular	**C** fantastic	**D** general
1 **A** deal	**B** load	**C** extent	**D** pile
2 **A** richly	**B** warmly	**C** deeply	**D** sharply
3 **A** ordinary	**B** simple	**C** usual	**D** normal
4 **A** Either	**B** Whether	**C** Wherever	**D** However
5 **A** absolutely	**B** actively	**C** strongly	**D** fully
6 **A** step	**B** section	**C** detail	**D** point
7 **A** Even	**B** Although	**C** Yet	**D** Still
8 **A** raise	**B** enhance	**C** heighten	**D** thrive

EXAM TIP

Check if the options collocate with any of the words surrounding the gap.

WRITING
A REVIEW

» SEE *PREPARE TO WRITE* BOX, STUDENT'S BOOK PAGE 49

1 Make notes to answer the following questions.

1 Have you ever been on an organised bike tour of a city with a guide? Which city was it? What did you see? Did you enjoy it?

_____

_____

_____

2 If you haven't, would you like to go on a bike tour like that? Why do you think you would / would not enjoy it?

_____

_____

_____

_____

2 Write down three positive things about going on a city bike tour and three negative things.

_____

_____

_____

_____

_____

3 Read the task. What questions do you have to answer about the tour?

> On a recent holiday, you went on a city bike tour in a group with a guide. An international travel website has asked you to write a review of the tour, commenting on whether you enjoyed it, how well it was organised and the kind of person the city bike tour is most suitable for. Explain why you would or wouldn't encourage other visitors to the city to go on this tour.
> Write your **review** in 220–260 words.

_____

_____

_____

4 Read the review of a bike tour in Barcelona, a city in Catalonia, Spain. Ignore the gaps. What answers are given to the questions from Exercise 3?

🚲   HOME | REVIEWS | NEWS   ☰

More ▾   Search   🔍

I recently went for a week's holiday in Barcelona, and one of the highlights of the trip for me was a half-day city bike tour. It was hugely enjoyable and, ¹ _____, extremely well-run.

We met outside the tour organisers' office at 11 o'clock – not too early, which worked for me! We then spent the next four hours visiting the city, stopping every few hundred metres or so to take photographs of some absolutely stunning sights, and hear clear and concise information about their history from Jordi, our very knowledgeable guide. There was a short stop for lunch halfway through the tour, though ² _____ the price of the meal was not included.

It ³ _____ the tour is suitable for people of all ages. We cycled at a relaxed pace, on easy-to-ride bikes with comfortable seats. The route we took included no hills, and ⁴ _____ was that we sometimes had to get off our bikes and walk through particularly busy areas.

I would encourage anyone able to ride a bike to go on one of these tours. The guide did a fantastic job, giving us useful tips and suggestions for what to see and do during the rest of our stay in the city. ⁵ _____ book in advance, as these tours are extremely popular. Based ⁶ _____, I can thoroughly recommend this bike trip as a great way to have fun, get some exercise and meet other people, while learning about one of the world's most fascinating cities.

★★★★☆   👍 Helpful?

_____

_____

5 Complete the review in Exercise 4 with the options in the box. Add capital letters where necessary.

> it is essential to   it is worth noting that
> on my experience   seems to me that
> the only downside   to my mind

6 Complete the other reviews for bike tours with the words in the box. Use capital letters where necessary.

> blast   clockwork   coat   doubt   fair   found   ~~frankly~~   frustrating   hopefully   missed   utterly

This was, **quite** ⁰ *frankly* , the worst morning of my holiday. It really was pretty awful. Admittedly, I'm not particularly fit, but we should have been warned about all the steep hills we'd have to climb. By the end, I was ¹ _____ **exhausted**. ² _____ , this review will serve as a useful warning to those who, like me, prefer to go sightseeing in a more relaxed manner.

Read more reviews ▾

★★★☆☆ 654 reviews

Everything **worked like** ³ _____ , from the moment we all met to the time when, four hours later, we said our goodbyes, agreeing that we'd all **had a** ⁴ _____ . I think **it's** ⁵ _____ **to say that**, despite their offices looking as if they were **in need of a** ⁶ _____ **of paint**, this bike tour company has hit on a winning formula.

💬 5   ♡ 20   ⇄ 9

NEWS | **REVIEWS** | FEATURED

 What I ⁷ _____ **was** that, **without a** ⁸ _____ , it had been worth my while reading up on the sights before actually seeing them; it was so windy that it was often hard to catch what our guide was saying. We also ⁹ _____ **out on** a couple of interesting places because, unfortunately, they were closed that day. For people who were leaving the following morning, this was **intensely** ¹⁰ _____ .

 Reviews (579)

7 Complete the sentences with one of the words or phrases in bold in Exercise 6.

1 Although I can't say it was the most fun I've ever had, it was, _____ , very enjoyable.
2 It was a shame that we _____ seeing the street market, but it couldn't be helped.
3 The funfair was thrilling, even though some of the rides looked a bit neglected and clearly _____ .
4 We thanked the tour operators for a great weekend. We _____ , and would definitely go back!
5 The tour would appeal to people who are a little bit more energetic than I am. I was _____ afterwards!
6 This tour was organised very efficiently – it all _____ .

8 Read the review question. What kind of course are you going to write about? What positive things are you going to say? Are you going to say anything negative?

> You see the following announcement on a website for young people.
>
> Have you spent a weekend, a day or half a day doing an activity course? It could be a sports course, an art course or something else. Write a review, explaining to what extent your expectations of the course were fulfilled and whether any aspects of it could have been improved. Explain how suitable you think it would be for other people your age.
>
> Write your **review** in 220–260 words.

✓ **PREPARE FOR THE EXAM**

Writing Part 2

9 Write your review, using some of the words and phrases you have learned. Write 220–260 words.

✓ **EXAM TIP**

Keep your target reader in mind as you write – make sure that you are providing information that is potentially useful to the reader.

VOCABULARY AND READING
LANDSCAPE

1 Complete the sentences with the words in the box.

> alleyway coastline cove flyover landmark
> landowner rocky scenic summit underpass
> vegetation

1 The entrance to the café was down a pretty little _____ off the main street.
2 They cleared away a lot of _____ in order to build this huge car park.
3 They built a _____ so the two motorways could cross.
4 The castle is the most famous _____ in our town.
5 Be careful, the path's quite _____ – don't fall over!
6 They managed to climb to the _____, despite the bad weather.
7 Don't try to cross this busy road on foot – use the _____ instead.
8 If you want to camp by the river, you'll need to get permission from the _____ first.
9 If you're going to drive, I'd recommend taking the _____ route, following the _____.
10 You could even stop and swim in a quiet, sandy _____ along the way.

2 Match the definitions to the words in Exercise 1.

A the person that a field or other area of land belongs to _____
B a bridge that carries a road over another road _____
C rough and difficult to travel along because of rocks _____
D the highest point of a mountain _____
E a curved part of a coast surrounding an area of water _____
F a path that goes under a busy road for pedestrians or cyclists to use _____
G the shape of the land next to the sea _____
H plants in general, or plants found in a particular area _____
I having or showing beautiful natural features _____
J a narrow road or path between buildings _____
K a place or a building that is easily recognised _____

3 Read the first paragraph of the article on the opposite page, ignoring the gaps. Which of the following sentences is true?

A The journey started in 2016.
B The project's aims were achieved.
C There were no problems during the flight.

 PREPARE FOR THE EXAM

Reading and Use of English Part 1

4 Read the first paragraph again. Decide which answer (A, B, C or D) best fits each gap.

	A	B	C	D
0	took	made	went	kept
1	stretches	ranges	spreads	distances
2	way	means	doubt	sooner
3	repetitive	reliable	renewable	recycled
4	faulty	grumpy	shabby	bumpy
5	leaving	getting	sending	causing
6	incredible	legendary	extraordinary	prestigiou
7	boost	relief	value	aid
8	significantly	limitlessly	utterly	fully

(answer 0 B made is circled)

 EXAM TIP

Learn phrases that may be tested at this level (e.g. *by no means*), and use them when you are speaking or writing.

5 Read the rest of the article and answer the questions.

1 Apart from benefiting the environment, how does Piccard say clean technologies make the world better?
2 How did the pilot save energy during the night?
3 Did the weather affect the speed of the plane?
4 What was the main thing that prevented the pilots from flying round the world all in one go?
5 How long did it take for Piccard to be allowed to be in charge of a plane?
6 What other record set by Piccard is mentioned?
7 Who does Piccard give credit to for helping him achieve his goal?

6 Match the highlighted words or phrases in the text to the definitions.

1 make good use of _____
2 moved through the air without any power _____
3 in a way that earns money _____
4 breaking by a long way _____
5 stage _____

FIRST SOLAR PLANE TO COMPLETE A round-the-world TRIP

On 26th July 2016, the solar-powered plane Solar Impulse 2 **(0)** _made_ history by completing the first round-the-world solar-powered flight, starting and finishing in Abu Dhabi, in the United Arab Emirates. It had flown over **(1)** _____ of scenic coastline, picturesque coves, rocky summits and no **(2)** _____ some famous landmarks, too. The flight aimed to demonstrate the potential of **(3)** _____ energy. The final stage was **(4)** _____, with turbulence driven by hot desert air **(5)** _____ the solo pilot, Bertrand Piccard, struggling with the controls.

The now **(6)** _____ plane, carrying over 17,000 solar cells on its wings, began the circumnavigation in March 2015. It crossed the Pacific and Atlantic Oceans without the **(7)** _____ of fossil fuel, and spent more than 23 days in the air. Speaking to journalists from the cockpit shortly before landing, Piccard appeared **(8)** _____ delighted as he neared the end of the journey: 'It's a very, very special moment. I hope people will understand that it's not just a first in the history of aviation, but also a first in the history of energy.'

'All the clean technologies we use, they can be used everywhere. So, we've flown 40,000 km, but now it's up to other people to take it further. It's up to every person in a house to take it further, every head of state, every mayor in a city, every entrepreneur or company director. These technologies can make the world much better, and we have to use them, not only for the environment, but also because they're profitable and create jobs.'

During daylight, the solar panels charged the plane's batteries, which made up a quarter of the craft's 2.3 tonne weight. The pilot also climbed to nearly 9,000 m during the day, and glided down to 1,500 m at night to conserve power. The plane flew at about 50 km/h, although it could go faster when the sun was bright. The plane could have flown almost non-stop, but the pilots could not, due to the very demanding conditions aboard. Piccard alternated with André Borschberg to fly the 16 stages of the journey, spending up to five days in the unheated and unpressurised cabin, taking only brief naps.

Borschberg flew the longest leg, 6,500 km over the Pacific from Japan to Hawaii, smashing the record for the longest uninterrupted journey in aviation history.

But Piccard said his biggest challenge had been getting his pilot's licence in the first place. 'The challenge was to come from the world of ballooning and hang gliding to the world of aeroplanes and instruments and procedures. When I initiated the project, I had no aeroplane licence, so I had to work for it over six years. I did hundreds of hours to be allowed to fly a prototype aeroplane.'

Piccard and Borschberg, both Swiss, were experienced adventurers. Piccard had made the first non-stop balloon flight around the world in 1999, while Borschberg, a former Swiss Air Force pilot, had had brushes with death involving an avalanche and a helicopter crash. Piccard said the final leg from Cairo to Abu Dhabi was particularly tough because of the turbulence, and had to fly at a high altitude to avoid the worst of it. There were moments during that last night when he could not rest at all because he was so busy struggling with his flight controls. He said his ground team had made the record-breaking flight possible: 'I was alone in the plane, but all the people who have worked on this project are people who are completely devoted and committed to success. I'll give each of them a big hug because they made my dream possible.'

The aim of the Solar Impulse adventure was not to develop solar-powered planes for widespread use, but to show the capabilities of renewable energy. 'I worked for 15 years to have this demonstration of the improvements of these technologies, so now I really want to leverage this demonstration and create a world council for clean technologies,' Piccard said. 'That will allow all these experts and specialists to advise the governments and big corporations on which types of technology to use to profitably fight climate change and profitably protect the environment.'

GRAMMAR
CONDITIONALS AND CONJUNCTIONS

1 Choose the correct options.

1 The navigation system works well as long as there *is / will be* a strong signal.

2 I wouldn't *reach / have reached* the summit if it hadn't been for the guide's expert help.

3 If it *wasn't / isn't* for the fact that his father was the company director, he would never have got the job.

4 Provided that these directions are correct, we *will / would* arrive at our destination in about an hour.

5 Even if it *was / is* legal, I would never be a graffiti artist.

6 Whether or not you *enjoy / would enjoy* beaches, you have to admit this little cove is wonderful.

7 Supposing all the mobile networks failed at the same time, how *would / did* people react?

8 But for the fact that I always carry a compass, we *never / 'd never* have made it back to camp before dark.

2 Match the correct conditional to the sentences 1–8 in Exercise 1.

A zero conditional ....

B first conditional ....

C second conditional ....

D third conditional ....

E mixed conditional ....

3 Choose the correct conjunction to complete the sentences.

1 As it is a completely new story, viewers will enjoy this second series .... they have seen the first.

  A unless   B whether or not   C supposing

2 .... an emergency, please leave the building in an orderly manner.

  A In the event of   B Assuming   C Providing

3 You won't be allowed in after 8 pm .... you have a valid ticket.

  A supposing   B even if   C provided that

4 .... the kindness of a passing stranger, I wouldn't have been able to pay the taxi fare.

  A Provided   B Unless   C But for

5 Anyone is welcome to join the expedition .... that they have some climbing experience.

  A providing   B in case of   C supposing

6 .... that I pass my driving test, I'm going to drive to Scotland this spring.

  A In the event of   B Unless   C Assuming

7 Agriculture will suffer worldwide .... something is done about global warming.

  A unless   B provided   C only if

8 .... there's no wi-fi in the hotel, how would upload your photos?

  A Even if   B Supposing   C As long as

9 We still have time to save the planet, but .... we act now.

  A only if   B unless   C in the event of

10 Please read the instructions regarding what to do .... a fire.

  A even if   B in case of   C supposing

 ## 4 Correct the mistakes in the sentences or put a tick by any you think are correct.

1 Unless carbon emissions are not reduced, pollution will become dangerous. ....

2 If early humans wouldn't have discovered agriculture, civilisation would be very different today.
....

3 If only they hadn't built that factory here, this would be quite scenic. ....

4 Provided it had enough charge, your GPS will get you to your destination safely. ....

5 If I'd got better grades in my exams, I wouldn't be working here now. ....

6 The flight won't be able to leave on time unless the weather doesn't improve. ....

 ## PREPARE FOR THE EXAM

Reading and Use of English Part 4

5 Complete the second sentence so that it has a similar meaning to the first sentence, using the word given. Do not change the word given. You must use between three and six words, including the word given.

1 You can borrow my mobile if you promise not to lose it.
LONG
I'll .... as you promise not to lose it.

2 Whether or not you support me, I am running this race tomorrow.
EVEN
I am running this race tomorrow .... me your support.

3 Supposing an accident happened, what action would you take?
EVENT
What would you .... an accident?

4 The only way he won't win is if an opponent trips him up again.
UNLESS
He won't .... by an opponent again.

5 If they have revised thoroughly, they have nothing to worry about.
PROVIDING
They have nothing to worry about, ... thorough.

6 I only got home safely that night because of a kind stranger.
BEEN
If it .... of a stranger, I'd never have got home safely that night.

EXAM TIP

There are two points for each item, so check your answer has made at least two changes to the structure of the original sentence.

VOCABULARY
HOMOPHONES, HOMONYMS, HOMOGRAPHS

1 Complete the sentences with the words in brackets.

1 I needed some _____ and quiet so that I could practise playing a _____ by Mozart on my violin. (piece / peace)

2 The _____ of money I spend on food every month is huge, but I can still save _____ for other things. (some / sum)

3 If you want to _____ your cooking ingredients accurately, the best _____ to do it is with kitchen scales. (way / weigh)

4 You are not _____ to read _____ in the library, because it disturbs others. (aloud / allowed)

5 Older people often say that time _____ more slowly in the _____. (passed / past)

6 The _____ was flat and treeless – so an ideal place for landing the _____. (plane / plain)

7 _____ some cheese and mix it with garlic mayonnaise to make a _____ sandwich! (great / grate)

8 I couldn't _____ my ID card, so I was _____ by the police. (find / fined)

9 We woke up the next morning when we _____ a _____ of cows walking past our tent. (herd / heard)

10 Do you know _____ the _____ will be calm enough for hot-air ballooning tomorrow? (whether / weather)

2 Choose the correct options.

1 I was distressed to see my bruise had *grown / groan* bigger overnight.

2 Why do you always *chews / choose* the same flavour ice cream?

3 The chemical symbol for *led / lead* is Pb.

4 She was thrilled to be given the *roll / role* of Lady Macbeth in the school play.

5 Fortunately, the *plane / plain* provided a perfect place for the pilot to make an emergency landing.

6 It was such an enormous doughnut that I wasn't able to eat the *hole / whole* thing.

7 We watched the filming of a *seen / scene* for a popular sitcom outside our building.

8 These digital scales are the best *way / weigh* to keep track of how many kilos you have lost.

9 I love to relax at the end of the day by playing a gentle *piece / peace* of music on my piano.

10 This dessert tastes even better if you *grate / great* some nutmeg over it.

3 Match the word in bold to the definitions.

1 Sleeping on a **hard** floor is not a pleasant experience.

2 The exam wasn't as **hard** as I thought it would be.

3 My **current** situation means that I don't have much free time.

4 Don't go swimming in the sea at the moment because there's a strong **current**.

5 He's so **mean** – he bought his wife a £1 bar of chocolate for her birthday.

6 The new factory will **mean** more jobs in the area.

7 All my important documents are kept in a **safe**.

8 Are you sure pedestrians will be **safe** when all cars are driverless?

a ungenerous
b a strong box with special locks used for storing valuables
c result in
d difficult
e happening at the present time
f not in danger
g not soft
h movement of water or electricity in a particular direction

1 ____ 3 ____ 5 ____ 7 ____
2 ____ 4 ____ 6 ____ 8 ____

4 Is the pronunciation of the words in bold the same (*S*) or different (*D*)?

0 She is the **kind** of person who is always **kind** to animals. _S_

1 Would you **object** if I threw this ugly **object** in the bin? ____

2 There is just a **minute** amount of dirt, so it should only take a **minute** to clean. ____

3 A surgeon who has saved the **lives** of hundreds of people **lives** next door to me. ____

4 The next time I go on a coach **trip**, I'll try not to **trip** over when I arrive at our destination. ____

5 I put on what I thought was a clean shirt, but I didn't **spot** the dirty **spot** on the collar. ____

6 I'm sorry, I didn't **mean** to suggest you were being **mean**. ____

7 Drinking water which contains **lead** can **lead** to serious health problems. ____

8 The storm is getting really **close** now, so we'd better **close** all the windows. ____

5 Which words do the words in bold rhyme with?

1 She was in the **lead** for the first half of the race, but then dropped back.
need / shed

2 My twin brother and I have a very **close** relationship.
chose / dose

3 At the end of a play, it is customary for the actors to return to the stage and **bow** to the audience.
toe / now

4 It only takes a **minute** amount of electricity to power a mobile phone.
fine / bin

5 I bought my little nephew a **wind**-up toy for his birthday.
find / pinned

6 It is difficult to estimate how many **lives** were saved by the vaccine.
gives / dives

LISTENING

1 Look at the pictures. What are they? Why would somebody buy one?

2 What problems do you think someone might have with these things?

3 Look at the two tasks in Exercise 5 and underline the key words.

4 Match the words and phrases to the definitions.
1 operating instructions ....
2 acquaintance ....
3 flaw ....
4 incur unforeseen expenses ....
5 obsession ....

a something that you think about all the time
b fault
c manual
d someone you know
e unexpectedly have to pay a fee or charge

✓ PREPARE FOR THE EXAM

Listening Part 4

 5 You'll hear five short extracts in which people are talking about technological devices they have bought.

TASK ONE

For questions 1–5, choose from the list (A–H) the reason each person gives for buying the device.

A a change in the workplace
B the enthusiasm of an acquaintance
C a desire for self-improvement
D a hunger for new experiences
E a need to acquire useful skills
F a requirement to complete an assignment
G a concern for the environment
H a compulsion to keep up with recent developments

1 Speaker 1 ....
2 Speaker 2 ....
3 Speaker 3 ....
4 Speaker 4 ....
5 Speaker 5 ....

TASK TWO

For questions 6–10, choose from the list (A–H) the problem each speaker had with the item.

A It quickly lost its initial attraction.
B It lacked clear operating instructions.
C It caused a feeling of anxiety.
D It required too frequent updates.
E It became an unhealthy obsession.
F It ceased to be useful.
G It suffered from a technical flaw.
H It incurred unforeseen expenses.

6 Speaker 1 ....
7 Speaker 2 ....
8 Speaker 3 ....
9 Speaker 4 ....
10 Speaker 5 ....

✓ EXAM TIP

The answers can come at the beginning, middle or end of each speaker's turn.

 6 Listen one more time. Do the answers for each speaker come at the beginning (B), middle (M) or end (E)?

Speaker 1: 1 ....   6 ....
Speaker 2: 2 ....   7 ....
Speaker 3: 3 ....   8 ....
Speaker 4: 4 ....   9 ....
Speaker 5: 5 ....   10 ....

READING AND USE OF ENGLISH

1 Look at the example item (0) in Exercise 4. Are any of these options possible?

A previously   **B** past   **C** away

2 Choose the correct option to complete the sentence.

I have never met *so / such* an amusing person as Simon.

3 Why is the other option incorrect?

....

....

PREPARE FOR THE EXAM

Reading and Use of English Part 2

4 Read the text below and think of the word which best fits each gap. Use only one word in each gap. There is an example at the beginning (0).

The best
INVENTION

About a century **(0)** *ago* , the English science-fiction writer H.G. Wells said, 'When I see an adult on a bicycle, I **(1)** .... longer despair of the human race.' In the years since the Industrial Revolution, the world has seen an explosion of technical inventiveness, but none has had **(2)** .... an exclusively positive effect as the bicycle.

Nearly every modern invention has its downside, **(3)** .... from the bicycle. The car pollutes our cities, the TV spreads fake news, the computer shortens our attention span, etc. But, **(4)** .... or not you are a cyclist yourself, it is difficult to **(5)** .... up with a single drawback of this 18th-century invention.

As **(6)** .... as energy consumption is concerned, it is a more efficient method of travel than walking. Needless to **(7)** ...., the car is way behind in this respect. A litre of petrol will drive you about 16 km, whereas if you use the energy equivalent of that litre to pedal a bicycle, you will travel over 1,000 km, as **(8)** .... as you are fit enough!

5 Look at the example item (0) in Exercise 9. What part of speech is it? What part of speech is the root word in capitals on the right?

....

6 Look at items (1)–(8). What part of speech are the root words on the right?

1	3	5	7 ....
2	4	6	8 ....

7 Now look again at the items (1)–(8). What part of speech is required for each?

1	3	5	7 ....
2	4	6	8 ....

8 Which two items in Exercise 9 require an opposite?

....

PREPARE FOR THE EXAM

Reading and Use of English Part 3

9 Read the text below. Use the word given in capitals at the end of some of the lines to form a word that fits in the gap in the same line.

Wind farms

Wind farms are an **(0)** *increasingly* common sight around the world.	**INCREASE**
Onshore wind farms are built in areas which are **(1)** .... windy, such as hillsides. They are one of the most effective	**SPECIAL**
ways of producing **(2)** .... energy. 75 percent less expensive than solar power, and even slightly cheaper than nuclear power, onshore wind is also a winner as far as	**RENEW**
cost **(3)** .... is concerned.	**EFFICIENT**
There are, however, problems associated with wind farms. One of them is the notorious **(4)** .... of their	**RELY**
source of energy – the wind – which does not always blow. **(5)** ....,	**ADD**
they can have a negative impact on the surrounding countryside, and sometimes produce noise. This has led to protests by local **(6)**	**RESIDE**
One way of avoiding these problems is to build the wind farms offshore – in the middle of the sea – where the wind blows more constantly. The countryside is left completely **(7)** ...., and there's nobody to complain.	**SPOIL**
The trouble is, building huge wind farms miles out at sea is unsurprisingly expensive, and once built, repair and **(8)** .... is also costly.	**MAINTAIN**

✓ EXAM TIP

Read the whole text first! Some answers can be found by looking at the words surrounding the gap, while others require an understanding of the whole paragraph or text.

✓ EXAM TIP

If a verb is required, think about what form is needed. Also, think about what tense is required, and whether it should be singular or plural.

VOCABULARY AND READING
CELEBRITY

1 Choose the correct options.

1 It certainly *hit the headlines / hit the public* when three of the most famous film stars decided to stop using their cars and cycle everywhere instead!

2 There were several *A-list celebrities / name celebrities* at the party.

3 It's important for politicians to have *appearance / credibility*, otherwise no one will trust them.

4 Do you think that actors should *aspire / endorse* politicians, or should they keep their preferences to themselves?

5 Our country's most famous novelist is going to make a rare *public appearance / public spotlight*.

6 The *sneaker / stalker* was arrested outside the singer's house, and will appear in court next month.

7 Some people tried to *sneak into / stalk into* the concert without paying, but they were caught and thrown out.

8 A lot of *big names / big headlines* trained at this drama school.

9 You should always *aspire to / endorse to* be the best person you can be!

10 It must be tiring for celebrities to be *in the appearance / in the spotlight* all the time.

2 Match the definitions to the words and expressions in Exercise 1. One definition has two answers.

A very famous people ....
B enter secretly ....
C receiving a lot of public attention ....
D show public approval or support ....
E have an ambition to achieve something or be successful ....
F appear in the news suddenly, or receive lots of attention in news outlets ....
G someone who illegally follows or watches someone over a period of time ....
H the fact that someone can be believed ....
I an occasion when someone is seen by a lot of people ....

3 Complete the sentences with the correct words or expressions from Exercise 1.

1 If people who are .... celebrities don't make a .... for weeks, people start wondering if they're ill.

2 Everyone should .... to something, even if it isn't anything very ambitious.

3 Make sure nobody can .... the building after the filming has begun.

4 Stars who are nearly always .... need a bit of privacy in their lives.

5 The cast and crew heard the news before it ....

6 When celebrities .... things like shampoo, they need to use these products themselves, or they'll lose ....

7 The actor was relieved when the .... was identified and caught.

8 With all those big .... in it, the film should be good!

4 Read the first paragraph of the article on the opposite page, ignoring the gaps. What does Kayla say about her future ambitions?

A She is certain she has made the right choice of career.
B She continues to hope that she will become a celebrity.
C She would like to carry on doing what she has always done.

PREPARE FOR THE EXAM

Reading and Use of English Part 8

5 You are going to read an article in which four young people write about their relationship with celebrities. For questions 1–10, choose from the writers (A–D). The writers may be chosen more than once.

Which person mentions

1 embracing ideas promoted by a celebrity? ....
2 collaborating with someone who is now a celebrity? ....
3 anticipating a possible meeting with a celebrity? ....
4 associating a celebrity with feelings of security? ....
5 being unexpectedly complimented by a celebrity? ....
6 confusing one celebrity with another? ....
7 reconsidering their attitude towards a celebrity? ....
8 imitating a celebrity's gestures? ....
9 contradicting a celebrity without intending to? ....
10 relating to a celebrity's problems? ....

EXAM TIP

Read the questions and underline the key words and phrases in each one.

6 Match the highlighted words or phrases in the text to the definitions.

1 become familiar and relaxed in a new place ....
2 possible reason for being well-known ....
3 basic fact ....
4 face to face ....
5 new way ....

Celebrities and me

A Kayla

When I was little, I used to watch a well-known singer's music videos over and over again. I observed every single move she made really carefully, and then I'd try to reproduce them as precisely as I could. I must have looked quite funny, but at the time I thought I was just so cool. Then I started making my own music videos and uploading them, but they didn't make me a star. I did create a couple of videos with another kid, who's now gone on to be very successful – I don't think she'd remember me because we only ever met online, but it's my small claim to fame! I suppose I still do aspire to be a big name one day, but I've accepted that my talents probably lie elsewhere – I don't think I'd ever succeed in the music industry. I'm looking into possibly working in films, maybe as a producer. In the meantime, what I'm really focusing on is my studies.

B Garth

Once, when I was in a chatroom for fans of an actor from my country, I said something about my town being pretty dull, only to find out later that, a few hours before my post, the actor had been going on about what a fascinating place it was. Apparently, he'd spent a day here the year before, and knew quite a lot about my town's history. I wasn't so much embarrassed as annoyed I'd missed the chance to see him in the flesh. Another time, I posted a poem about a singer on her fan site, and she said it was outstanding. I hadn't imagined she'd ever actually bother to read it! I follow lots of famous people on social media, and it's great that some of them are happy to chat to fans like me, which is always a thrill! I'm surprised any of them have time, or even care about what people like me think, but I suppose the bottom line is that fans like me are an intrinsic part of their success – though not all A-listers appreciate that.

C Berit

I try not to be obsessive about it, but I am very interested in celebrities and their lives. I think it started when I used to sit with my parents and watch a pop singer they particularly loved on TV. Whenever I see or read anything about that star now, it brings back those times, when I was convinced nothing could ever harm me as long as I was with my mum and dad. As I got older, I became interested in environmental issues, and it was partly because that singer was, too. He did a lot of good work raising awareness about things like clean energy and reducing plastic waste, and endorsed politicians who were concerned about these things, too. I must admit, I was disappointed when I discovered that he spent a lot of time flying around in his private jet, even using it to go and speak at conferences about saving the planet. For me, that meant he lost a lot of credibility, and I saw him in a different light after that.

D Simon

I read quite a lot about sports stars, especially footballers. Apart from being amazing at what they do and really dedicated, they also have to be very adaptable, as they move from team to team and from city to city. One of my favourite footballers has talked about how hard that can be. When I moved to the town where I live now, it took me a while to settle in, so I have an idea of how it feels. It must be even worse when you're constantly in the spotlight. Last month, there were rumours he'd be coming to the opening of a big new sports stadium in my area. Apart from on the football field, he doesn't make that many public appearances, so I went there hoping I might get a selfie with him. In the end, though, a famous athlete came instead, and for a moment, from behind, I thought it was my hero. Then he turned around and I realised my mistake.

GRAMMAR
RELATIVE CLAUSES

1 Choose the correct options.

1 Getting endorsed by an A-list celebrity is something *who / that* many up-and-coming bands aspire to.
2 Method acting is the type of acting *which / whereby* the actor tries to experience the emotions of the character.
3 For our project about publicity-shy celebrities, we contacted several big names, none of *whom / who* replied.
4 When she was a teenager, the actress Judy Garland came into the spotlight, *where / which* she remained for the rest of her life.
5 He is the kind of politician *which / whose* public appearances do little to enhance his credibility.
6 As a child, I sneaked into a lot of films, some of *which / whom* were much too scary for me.
7 Winning an Academy Award is something *which / who* most actors will never experience.
8 The novel *that / where* the film was based on is now out of print.

2 Complete the rules with the sentences 1–8 in Exercise 1.

A Which of the sentences contain defining relative clauses?

B Which contain non-defining relative clauses? ....

C Which contain a relative pronoun that can be omitted?

D Which contain formal relative clause constructions?

3 Complete the second sentences with *of which, of whose* or *of whom* and a quantity word from the box.

> all (x2)   ~~both~~   few   most   neither   none

0 I have two brothers. They are actors.
  I have two brothers, *both of whom* are actors.
1 He loves Judy Garland. He has seen every one of her films.
  He loves Judy Garland, ... films he has seen.
2 She tried on several rings, but they were all too small.
  She tried on several rings, ... fitted her.
3 The majority of celebrities I have met are insecure.
  I have met many celebrities, ... are insecure.
4 Many people have been contestants on reality TV shows. A few of them have become famous.
  Reality TV shows have had many contestants, a .... have become famous.
5 We saw two plays at the festival, but they weren't any good.
  We saw two plays at the festival, ... were any good.
6 Every film this director made was a masterpiece.
  This director made several films, ... were masterpieces.

PARTICIPLE CLAUSES

4 Complete the sentences with the verbs in brackets in the correct participle form.

1 The park wall full of people .... the sunshine. (enjoy)
2 Half of the audience, ... by the performance, got up and walked out. (disappoint)
3 We caught two teenagers .... into the stadium without tickets. (sneak)
4 Anyone .... to work in journalism should write for their college newspaper. (aspire)
5 All students .... less than a C in their essay must write it again. (give)
6 Any film .... by Bobby Hilton has been hugely successful. (endorse)
7 I like to read magazines .... in celebrity gossip. (specialise)
8 What was the name of that film .... on the true story of a mountain rescue? (base)

◉ 5 Correct the mistakes in the sentences or put a tick by any you think are correct.

1 Katherine Hepburn is the actress having won the most Academy Awards in history.

2 We went to a restaurant was less expensive and better than the one you suggested.

3 The speaker gave a quick plot summary for those whom had not seen the film. ....
4 The stress under which many performers are expected to work is incredible.

5 Reality TV shows are not something I'm really interested in them. ....
6 Detected the problem, the camera operator was ready to shoot the scene again.

6 Complete the sentences with the words in the box in the correct form.

> affect   chain   direct   drink   get   read
> take   wish

1 Anyone .... this blog will know that I am a huge fan of horror movies.
2 Passengers .... off at the next stop are advised to check that they have all their belongings with them.
3 .... a selfie with the lead singer, I immediately uploaded it to all my social media accounts.
4 Any bicycles .... to these gates will be removed by security.
5 Critics say the latest film .... by Tammy Wilcox is her best yet.
6 We apologise to anyone .... by this change in the schedule.
7 She felt very restless and energetic, ... four espressos.
8 Anyone .... to attend tonight's lecture must register before 5 pm today.

VOCABULARY
DEPENDENT PREPOSITIONS

1 Match the words to the definitions.

1 adviser		**6** knowledgeable	
2 central		**7** outbreak	
3 coverage		**8** misled	
4 engrossed		**9** portrayal	
5 impose		**10** sympathetic	

a showing understanding and concern
b force someone to accept something, or officially force a rule
c main or important
d giving all your attention to something
e the reporting of a particular event or subject
f the way that someone or something is described or represented in an artistic work
g someone whose job is to give advice
h made to believe something which is not true
i when something suddenly begins, especially a disease or something unpleasant
j knowing a lot

1		**3**		**5**		**7**		**9**	
2		**4**		**6**		**8**		**10**	

2 Which preposition usually follows the words in Exercise 1? Complete the table.

to	about	of
adviser		

on	in	over

3 Complete the conversations with the words in the boxes in the correct form and a preposition.

~~advise~~   centre   lead   portray

1 A: Have you heard? The chief *adviser to* the president has resigned.
  B: That's strange. I thought she was .... the organisation.
  A: She was, but she was annoyed about being .... educational reform.
  B: Are you sure it had nothing to do with the .... her as a fool in that newspaper article last week?

cover   gross   sympathy

2 A: I'm completely .... this book about celebrities living their lives in the spotlight. It's fascinating.
  B: I'm not very .... A-list celebrities who complain about their lack of privacy. What do they expect?
  A: Well, some of the .... their private lives in the press is pretty unfair.

4 Rewrite the sentences using a word + preposition from this page.

0 The history of cinema is a subject Sam knows very well.
Sam *is very knowledgeable about* the history of cinema.

1 This football match has really got my attention.
I .... this football match.

2 They led me to believe things about the job which weren't true.
I .... the nature of the job.

3 Sally has an extremely important role in this organisation.
Sally's .... this organisation.

4 I wish the homeless were shown more understanding and concern by the government.
I wish .... the homeless.

 PREPARE FOR THE EXAM

Reading and Use of English Part 3

5 Read the text below. Use the word given in capitals at the end of some of the lines to form a word that fits in the gap in the same line.

FAME AND HAPPINESS

Many people these days devote their lives to the pursuit of fame because they **(0)** *mistakenly* believe that it brings happiness.	**MISTAKE**
Perhaps it is modern society's **(1)** .... with celebrities which encourages us to think this way. Press and TV **(2)** .... of the lifestyles of the big names in Hollywood may provoke envy and longing. Their glamorous lives and **(3)** .... wealth is presented as the ultimate human achievement. But this, of course, is **(4)**	**OBSESS** **COVER** **IMAGINE** **LEAD**
Anyone **(5)** .... in the field of human behaviour – or indeed just the comings and goings of Hollywood high society – will tell you that the reality of those who live their lives in the spotlight is very different from the heavenly **(6)** .... you see in celebrity magazines and TV shows.	**KNOW** **PORTRAY**
The truth is, celebrities are often deeply unhappy.	
(7) .... to this claim is the fact that many famous people suffer from **(8)** .... and require constant reassurance. Unfortunately, nobody can control what other people think or say about you – so be careful what you wish for!	**CENTRE** **SECURE**

 EXAM TIP

Look at the words before and after the gap to help you decide what kind of word is required.

WRITING
A FORMAL EMAIL

» SEE *PREPARE TO WRITE* BOX, STUDENT'S BOOK PAGE 62

1 Make notes to answer the following questions.

   1 Would you like to be famous?

   ....

   ....

   2 If yes, what would you like to be famous for? What are the advantages of being famous?

   ....

   ....

   ....

   ....

   3 If no, why doesn't the idea of being famous appeal to you? What kinds of things about everyday life might be difficult for a celebrity?

   ....

   ....

   ....

   ....

2 Read the task. What points do you have to address?

> An online magazine recently published an article in which some celebrities complained about their quality of life, saying that fans make their lives impossible, and that they have to work too hard. You have read the article and think that the celebrities were being too negative. Write an email to the magazine editor, explaining why you disagree with the opinions expressed and saying what you feel are some of the benefits of being famous.
>
> Write your **email**.

....

....

....

3 Read the sample email to the editor, ignoring the gaps. Has the writer covered all the points in the task?

Dear Sir or Madam,

I have just read an article about celebrities in your magazine. Although it was interesting, I would like to respond ¹ .... some of the views expressed.

First of all, one claim in the article that I really take issue ² .... is that fans make celebrities' lives impossible. This seems to me to be a very sweeping statement and fails to take into account the obvious fact that without fans, these people would not be famous ³ .... the first place. Furthermore, I do not accept ⁴ .... a moment that the lifestyle of many A-list celebrities can be called 'impossible'. That is clearly not the case. I ⁵ .... one would love to be able to afford the luxuries that many big names seem to take ⁶ .... granted. I wonder whether some of the people quoted in the article have any awareness ⁷ .... how privileged they are.

As if this were not enough, several celebrities complained that they are overworked. Supposedly, they have more stressful lives than ordinary people. No evidence is provided to back ⁸ .... this allegation. Isn't it fair to say that most people in the world work hard and often experience a great deal ⁹ .... pressure every day? To be quite frank, it was disappointing to see such selfishness ¹⁰ .... display in the article and such a failure to recognise the undoubted advantages celebrities enjoy.

¹¹ .... my view, having financial security, being admired by many and seeing one's efforts rewarded is something to be appreciated. Celebrities should stop feeling sorry ¹² .... themselves.

Kind regards,

Alex Voltov

....

4 Complete the email in Exercise 3 with one word in each gap.

5 Look again at the sample email in Exercise 3. Underline words or phrases that the writer uses to do the following.

1 add points
2 summarise another person's opinion
3 use their own experience as an example
4 ask a rhetorical question
5 say that they don't think something is true
6 criticise an opinion

6 Choose the correct options.

1 *For / With / To* me personally, celebrities have no importance whatsoever.
2 This *carries / moves / brings* me to my next point, concerning the behaviour of some celebrities.
3 Nevertheless, *that / it / this* has to be said that some celebrities are excellent role models.
4 It wasn't *got / made / shown* clear what the writer has against fans who follow celebrities online.
5 The writer misrepresented the impact of fans *by / for / with* suggesting that this is always negative.
6 *For / Since / As* a 17-year-old myself, I don't recognise the writer's description of young people's online behaviour.
7 There are several points in the article that I *make / take / have* issue with.
8 The writer said that many fans end up stalking celebrities. That particular comment was *highly / greatly / rightly* misleading.
9 Lots of people enjoy reading about famous people. **After all, what is wrong** *for / with / of* that?
10 Singers often rely on their fans for moral support. **The same is** *correct / right / true* for many actors.
11 I do not believe that we are **anything** *just / like / close* as interested in A-list celebrities as they themselves think we are.
12 In addition, **there is** *no / never / not* reason to be unkind about people who are having some harmless fun.

7 Complete the sentences with an expression in bold from Exercise 5. Add punctuation and capital letters if necessary.

1 Everyone should work hard. Ordinary people should work hard, and _____ celebrities.
2 The article risks offending many young people _____ we are all staring at screens all day.
3 It is wrong to claim that the issue is _____ simple as implied in this article.
4 _____ critical of someone simply because they admire a famous person.
5 Many of us want to get a selfie with a celebrity, and _____ ?
6 _____ which is that modern life has left many people cut off from family and friends.
7 It was _____ of the reporter to claim that the singer was planning to leave the band.
8 Being in the spotlight is part of being a big name. However, _____ that many wish they could have more privacy.

8 Read the task. What points do you need to cover?

> You have read an article online about music festivals, saying that festivals nowadays are wonderful and much better than they used to be. In fact, you have been to some festivals recently which were not very enjoyable. For example, there were problems with sound quality, cancelled performances and the food. Write an email to the website editor, saying how you feel about your experiences.
> Write your **email**. Write 220–260 words.

 PREPARE FOR THE EXAM

Writing Part 2

9 Write your email, using some of the words and phrases you have learned. Write 220–260 words.

✓ EXAM TIP

Read the question carefully and decide what tone will be suitable for your response.

9 FIT AS A FIDDLE

VOCABULARY AND READING
HEALTH AND FITNESS

1 Complete the words in the sentences below. The first letter of each word is given.

1 If you don't do enough exercise, it will affect your w_____ -b_____. You'll feel less energetic, and your mood will suffer.

2 I feel so unfit! I'm not sure I'll ever g_____ b_____ i_____ s_____!

3 I was unlucky enough to p_____ a m_____ in my leg at the gym yesterday.

4 Some people worry about w_____ on their face, but I think they make you look wise.

5 Aerobics was a fitness c_____ in the 1990s – everyone was doing it.

6 Go for a swim – it will d_____ you t_____ w_____ o_____ g_____! You'll feel a thousand times better afterwards.

7 Running is a good way to b_____ o_____ calories.

8 Have you tried m_____ as a way of connecting to the present and forgetting about your problems for a while?

9 I use m_____ every day so my skin doesn't get too dry.

10 I think that having a warm shower is very t_____. It really helps me relax.

11 It takes a huge amount of s_____ to run a marathon. Imagine having to keep going for 42 kilometres!

12 Many of these fitness and diet f_____ are a bit of a waste of time, in my opinion. And they all disappear soon enough.

2 Match the definitions to a word or completed expression from Exercise 1.

1 something extremely popular for a limited period of time _____ or _____

2 make you healthy or make you feel much better _____

3 lines on the skin associated with age _____

4 the strength to do something difficult for a long time _____

5 the state of feeling healthy and happy _____

6 become fit again _____

7 a substance that you put on your skin to stop it from becoming dry _____

8 providing health and relaxation _____

9 injure a part of the body by stretching it too far or by tearing it _____

10 get rid of by doing exercise _____

11 being aware of your body, thoughts and feelings in the present moment _____

3 Read the first two paragraphs of the article on the opposite page, ignoring the gaps. How much did the writer pay to find out about high-intensity workouts? Why does she think that people are prepared to pay for them?

_____
_____

PREPARE FOR THE EXAM

Reading and Use of English Part 2

4 For questions 1–8, read the text on the opposite page and think of the word which best fits each gap. Use only one word in each gap. There is an example at the beginning (0).

EXAM TIP

If there's a verb after the gap, you may need to fill the gap with an auxiliary verb, such as *to be* or *can*.

5 Read the rest of the article and answer the questions.

Which activity does the writer say

1 contains some very demanding exercises? _____

2 has similar effects to those of another activity? _____

3 sometimes involves more thought than action? _____

4 appears to break accepted rules about fitness routines? _____

5 is worth doing in the company of others to begin with? _____

6 has been practised for a long time? _____

7 gives people little excuse not to do it? _____

8 requires a good level of fitness to do safely? _____

6 Match the highlighted words or phrases in the text to the definitions.

1 placed _____

2 what most people believe _____

3 avoiding doing something _____

4 very excited and full of energy _____

5 what is extremely clever about _____

TWO ROUTES
TO FITNESS

EXTREME HIGH-INTENSITY WORKOUTS

In normal life, I'm bad at saving money, but there are a few weird things I'm reluctant to splash out **(0)** _on_ . They include, but are **(1)** _____ limited to, the posh seats in cinemas and online workouts that charge a subscription fee. I'm really talking about some of the fitness programmes **(2)** _____ expense is an intrinsic part of the business model. When people pay high fees, they want to make sure they get **(3)** _____ money's worth, so they take the exercise programmes seriously; and when the participants are seen to be serious, this in turn attracts new customers. I still don't want to pay out, however.

Yet, **(4)** _____ way or another, these programmes have given rise **(5)** _____ free content being made in their image, which is **(6)** _____ I came upon a trainer who produces his own videos, and promises five-minute workouts that are as effective as half an hour's exercise. So, the way it works **(7)** _____ that all the exercises are twice as fast as you'd normally do them. On cardio day, it's extremely fast exercises and **(8)** _____ considerable (within the five-minute scope) amount of running on the spot. You definitely need stamina!

There are moves that are considerably harder than regular exercises. Chest and abdominals day has a *push-off*: from kneeling, you fall into a position in which you are lying face down, then push yourself up. You need a lot of abdominal engagement to even consider it, and it's still insanely hard. Try not to pull a muscle.

Conventional wisdom around fitness suggests you should have, more or less, equal amounts of activity and rest – that is, do one minute of high-intensity work, and then rest for 45 seconds. This, however, being only five minutes, is all high-intensity activity, and you have to think of the remainder of the day as your rest period.

The genius of this particular craze is that for those that want to get back into shape, there's no way of wriggling out of five minutes. It's nothing. You could lose that time looking for your phone. Or looking *at* your phone. Nobody's day is so packed that they cannot accommodate it, which is why – I guess – this fad promises to be at least as effective as a 30-minute ordinary workout. Anything that you regularly do will be more effective at burning off calories than something you intend to do, but don't.

TAI CHI

In England, tai chi used to be something you'd see people do in parks, two decades before anyone did aerobics or yoga there. The natural world is an important part of the practice. If you see a picture of someone doing tai chi, they are usually holding a pose on top of a mountain rock, with an amazing sunrise. Parks aren't normally as breathtaking as that, but they do have nature, and they are better than your living room.

I always thought tai chi looked ridiculous – the movements are so slight, smooth and odd. 'Move like the water that flows, without any hesitation,' instructs a tai-chi master on my screen. You simply couldn't mistake it for anything else, and to a busy, frenetic sort of person, it looks pointless.

But why am I so judgemental? It has a wide range of benefits, roughly aligned with those of yoga. It's good for sleep, flexibility, mood and weight loss. In an ideal world, you'd do it in a class, not because the moves are complicated, just because a teacher helps you do it at the correct pace. However, I started with an online tutorial and was amused by the terminology: *parting the wild horse's mane*, *separating the way the wild crane spreads its wings*.

The introduction will be familiar to anyone who has practised yoga, meditation or mindfulness. 'Learn how to feel. Learn how to stand,' the instructor summarises. I thought, 'Well, I already know how to stand, but learning how to feel could take years.'

'Close your eyes. Focus on how you breathe. Concentrate on your body, one part at a time. Feel the blood rushing into your hands. Concentrate harder.' Breathing correctly is just so vital, isn't it? You take three minutes out of your schedule to exhale more slowly and inhale more deeply, and wham, you're a different person – more present, less buzzing. It's certainly therapeutic.

It's a good few minutes before actual moving starts. One leg is lifted, infinitely slowly, at the knee, and planted a small distance away, before the arms come up. Again, the movements are so distinctive – in what other activity would you be flexing your hands up from the wrists, then back down again? But they don't process as exercise. It's more about well-being, learning how to feel, reconnecting with your body via the focus it takes to transition smoothly from one movement to another. Well, it may do me the world of good, but I was right – this could take years.

GRAMMAR
CLEFT STRUCTURES

1 Rewrite the sentences.

0 It was my younger brother who told me I needed to get into shape.
My _younger brother told me I needed to get into shape._

1 The reason she pulled a muscle was because she didn't warm up before exercising.
She pulled _____

2 What did him the world of good was learning how to meditate.
Learning _____

3 It's the wrinkles around your eyes that make you look older than you are.
You look _____

4 Something I love doing is burning off energy at the gym.
I love _____.

5 The one food that I cannot stand eating is liver.
I cannot _____.

2 Complete the sentences with the words in the box.

All	It was	One area where	The last
The person	The reason		

1 _____ in ancient China where the martial art of tai chi was developed.

2 _____ why I am so out of shape is that I keep getting injured.

3 _____ my health has improved since I started cycling is my stamina.

4 _____ thing he needs right now is you telling him to give up.

5 _____ I want to do right now is take a long break from the gym.

6 _____ who recommended I wear a fitness tracker was my personal trainer.

3 Make these sentences more emphatic by using a cleft structure.

1 I think a bit of sound healing is something you'd enjoy.
What _____.

2 Simon just wants to get back into shape.
All _____.

3 Stamina is one of the things I need to work on.
Something _____.

4 She became a champion cyclist by training incredibly hard.
It _____.

5 I never take my laptop to bed because it disturbs my sleep.
The reason _____.

4 Rewrite the sentences with a different emphasis each time.

0 A **doctor** advised **Greg** to take **mindfulness lessons**.
It was _a doctor who advised Greg to take mindfulness lessons._
It was _Greg who a doctor advised to take mindfulness lessons._
It was _mindfulness lessons that a doctor advised Greg to take._

1 **Sophia** does **power lifting** to **keep in shape**.
It is _____.
It is _____.
It is _____.

2 **Mario** injured his **back** at the **gym**.
_____

5 Correct the mistakes in the sentences or put a tick by any you think are correct.

1 It was I who pulled a muscle during training last night.

2 The reason he's not coming to class today because he's ill.

3 Something you should know about me is that I don't eat red meat.

4 The main thing that to remember is you must rest properly between sessions.

5 What I need to do is burning off some energy.

PREPARE FOR THE EXAM

Reading and Use of English Part 4

6 Complete the second sentence so that it has a similar meaning to the first sentence, using the word given. Do not change the word given. You must use between three and six words, including the word given.

1 He felt a good deal better after the therapeutic massage. **WORLD**
It was the therapeutic massage _____ good.

2 It's just the possibility of injuring myself that bothers me. **WORRIED**
The only _____ the possibility of injuring myself.

3 Not winning the tournament took us by surprise. **EXPECT**
What we _____ first in the tournament.

4 Laziness will not be tolerated by the team coach. **PUT**
Something the team coach refuses _____ laziness.

5 I admire and respect my PE teacher more than anyone. **LOOK**
The person _____ all is my PE teacher.

6 If you want to increase your strength, you could try lifting heavy weights. **STRONGER**
One _____ lift heavy weights.

 **EXAM TIP**

Look at the words around the gap and think about how they affect the words you need to use.

VOCABULARY
HEALTH IDIOMS

1 Match the two halves of the idioms.

1 fit as		a	your feet
2 off		b	hearing
3 a frog		c	in your throat
4 aches		d	a fiddle
5 the picture of		e	and pains
6 back on		f	colour
7 full		g	of beans
8 hard of		h	health

1 .... 3 .... 5 .... 7 ....
2 .... 4 .... 6 .... 8 ....

2 Complete the definitions with the idioms from Exercise 1.

1 If you look very well, people might say you are
....

2 Somebody who has a lot of energy is said to be
....

3 A person who exercises a lot and is in good shape is
....

4 When various parts of your body hurt, you are suffering from ....

5 If your complexion suggests that you are not well, you are looking ....

6 Somebody who has difficulty distinguishing sounds is
....

7 When you have recovered from an illness you can say you are ....

8 If your voice is affected by a cold or other infection, you sound like you have ....

HEALTH-RELATED ACTIONS

3 Choose the correct options to complete the sentences.

1 The only .... I was prescribed for my aches and pains was aspirin.
   A medication   **B** operation   **C** symptom

2 Hurry up, I don't want to .... my appointment.
   A take   **B** have   **C** miss

3 It was when she was running a marathon that she .... an injury.
   A contracted   **B** sustained   **C** took

4 I hope the chemist can give me something to alleviate these ....
   A medications   **B** symptoms   **C** treatments

5 What was the name of the specialist you .... about your back problem?
   A consulted   **B** contracted   **C** prescribed

6 What kind of .... did you have, and did it help?
   A symptom   **B** health   **C** treatment

7 I had to .... an operation to repair my broken ankle.
   A contract   **B** take   **C** have

8 It was in the Amazon rainforest that the explorer .... a rare illness.
   A contracted   **B** sustained   **C** underwent

4 Complete the conversations with words from this page.

1 **A:** Sammy .... a serious operation last month.
   B: Really, he looks fit as a .... now!

2 **A:** Take two of these pills three times a day to .... your symptoms.
   B: Sorry? How many did you say? I'm a bit .... of hearing.

3 **A:** I've been really suffering from aches and .... lately.
   B: Why don't you make an .... with the doctor? He might .... you some medication.

4 **A:** Are you OK? You look a bit off ....
   B: I'm fine. I've just got a frog in my ....

5 **A:** Did you hear? Maria sustained an .... playing football last weekend.
   B: Yes, I'm afraid it's going to be a few weeks before she's back on her ....

6 **A:** I had to consult a .... when I got back from holiday. Turns out I'd contracted an unusual ....
   B: Really? You look the picture of ....
   A: I know! And I feel full of .... , too!

5 Answer the questions so that they are true for you.

1 Are you as fit as a fiddle? Do you know anyone who is?
....

2 What were your symptoms the last time you were ill?
....

3 Were you prescribed any medicine?
....

4 Have you ever sustained an injury? What happened?
....

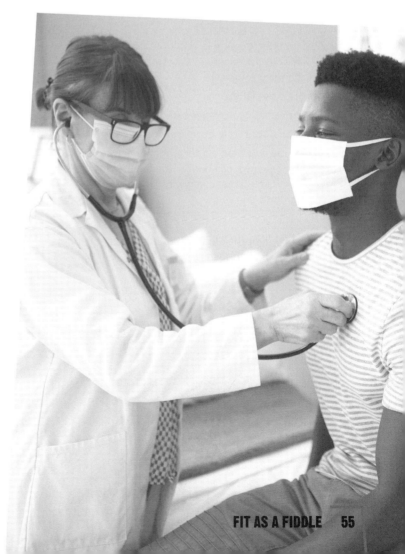

LISTENING

1 Look at questions 1–6 in Exercise 7 and answer the questions below.

1 What is the topic in each extract?

....

2 Are the conversations formal or informal?

....

2 Underline the key words in each question.

3 What is the focus of the questions 1–6 in Exercise 7? Choose from the categories in the box.

agreement   feeling   function/purpose

1	....	4	....
2	....	5	....
3	....	6	....

 4 Listen to Extract 1 and answer questions 1 and 2 in Exercise 7.

5 Now look at the first half of Extract 1. Underline the words that refer to:

1 the price
2 the number of people
3 the equipment

> **F:** Have you tried out the new gym in town yet?
>
> **M:** Yeah, I went yesterday. It was pretty packed, but they have a good range of gear, and there's plenty of space. Thirty pounds a month is a bit pricy, though.
>
> **F:** I thought it was reasonable. As you say, the facilities are excellent. What were the men's changing rooms like?
>
> **M:** Basic but functional.
>
> **F:** The ladies' were super clean.
>
> **M:** I was surprised at how many people were there.
>
> **F:** Maybe you went at the wrong time. I've been going in my lunch break, when it's quiet. How's your training going, anyway? Still doing that high-intensity stuff?

6 Now **highlight** the phrase that indicates agreement between the two speakers.

 PREPARE FOR THE EXAM

Listening Part 1

 7 You will hear three different extracts. For questions 1–6, choose the answer (A, B or C) which fits best according to what you hear. There are two questions for each extract.

Extract 1

You hear two friends talking about a new gym.

1 What do they think about the gym?
A It is overpriced.
B It is overcrowded.
C It is well equipped.

2 What motivates the man to continue his training programme?
A the satisfaction of having worked hard
B the effect it has on his physique
C the encouragement of a friend

Extract 2

You hear part of a radio interview with a nutrition researcher called Emma Beckett.

3 How does she feel about the public attitude to her work?
A frustrated by people who hold uninformed views on it
B surprised by the level of interest shown in it
C saddened by how many people ignore it

4 What is she doing when she talks about *superfoods*?
A criticising the poor-quality research about them
B advising scepticism about their supposed benefits
C encouraging listeners to find out about it themselves

Extract 3

You hear two old schoolfriends talking about school PE lessons.

5 They both believe that PE lessons
A are an essential part of education.
B can help students burn off excess energy.
C can lead to interesting career opportunities.

6 How does the man feel about their old PE teacher?
A appreciative of his sense of humour
B impressed by his athletic ability
C unconvinced by his teaching methods

EXAM TIP

If you are not sure about the correct answer, take a guess. You can usually eliminate at least one obviously wrong answer.

READING AND USE OF ENGLISH

1 Read the text in Exercise 5 quickly. What is mindfulness? What is the author's attitude towards it?

2 Now look at the example (0) in Exercise 5. Are any of the following possible as an alternative answer?

A many   **B** whole   **C** what

3 Which of the following are *not* possible for gap 1?

A named
B called
C such
D known
E which

4 Look at the sentence containing gap 2. What word after the gap gives you a clue to the answer?

 PREPARE FOR THE EXAM

Reading and Use of English Part 2

5 Read the text below and think of the word which best fits each gap. Use only one word in each gap. There is an example at the beginning (0).

Mindfulness

Of **(0)** *all* the health crazes which the 21st century has brought us, the phenomenon **(1)** _____ as mindful meditation, or *mindfulness*, is perhaps the most successful. Mindfulness is based on the ancient Buddhist path to enlightenment, but the focus has shifted **(2)** _____ achieving a blissful state of 'oneness' with the universe towards a more contemporary approach, where stress-relief and personal development take priority.

Although this modern adaptation of the traditional practice originated from someone knowledgeable **(3)** _____ Buddhism – a professor of medicine called Jon Kabat-Zinn – it rapidly grew into a multi-billion-dollar industry after **(4)** _____ adopted by some of the biggest corporations in Silicon Valley.

Today, there are over 70,000 books on mindfulness, all of **(5)** _____ are available to purchase. Alternatively, if reading is not your thing, you could splash **(6)** _____ on a luxury weekend retreat in an exotic location, **(7)** _____ you can learn all you need to know. Failing that, you can download one of the hundreds of apps dedicated **(8)** _____ keeping you mindful from dawn till dusk.

 EXAM TIP

When studying for this part of the exam, focus on verb forms, auxiliary and modal verbs, pronouns, prepositions, conjunctions, modifiers and determiners (e.g. *those, your, most*).

6 Choose the correct option.

You won't get back on your feet soon *unless / if only* you see a specialist.

7 Rewrite the sentence in Exercise 6.

The only way _____ .

8 Now look at the exam question. How would you complete it?

The only way she won't run in the marathon is if she is injured in training.

SUSTAINS

She will definitely run in the marathon _____ in training.

A if only she sustains an injury
B unless she sustains an injury
C unless she will sustain an injury

 PREPARE FOR THE EXAM

Reading and Use of English Part 4

9 Now complete the rest of the exam task. For questions 2–6, complete the second sentence so that it has a similar meaning to the first sentence using the word given. Do not change the word given. You must use between three and six words, including the word given.

2 All of the anti-wrinkle creams I tried were useless.
WHICH
I tried several anti-wrinkle creams, none _____ use at all.

3 'I've never had a therapeutic massage before,' said Chris
TIME
Chris said it was _____ a therapeutic massage.

4 There's a possibility that you will need to be operated on tomorrow.
UNDERGO
You _____ tomorrow.

5 He should consult a specialist for advice right now.
ABOUT
It _____ a specialist for advice.

6 Maria is never late for an appointment.
COUNT
You _____ on time for an appointment.

EXAM TIP

If you don't know the answer, make sure you write something. You might get one mark!

10 Each question in Part 4 of the *Reading and Use of English* section is worth two marks because you have to make two changes to the original sentence. Draw a line in your answers to Exercise 9 to separate the two changes you made.

1 *unless she sustains | an injury*

10 MAKE OR BREAK

VOCABULARY AND READING
CHALLENGES AND ACHIEVEMENTS

1 Complete the sentences with the words in the box in the correct form.

> bargain   gruelling   hang   lose   pay   pitfall
> rise   shot   track

1 When he rescued an injured snake, he got **more than he'd** _____ **for** when it bit him.

2 It's a real challenge, but I'm sure she'll _____ **to the occasion**.

3 They decided they **had nothing to** _____ by asking the farmer if they could camp in the field – there was nowhere else they could spend the night.

4 It's worth taking risks from time to time because sometimes they _____ **off**.

5 We may find someone in that small village who can help us fix the car, but it's **a long** _____ – I didn't see any garages.

6 Try to avoid the common _____ of getting stuck in traffic by setting off as early as possible.

7 She felt exhausted after a _____ run in the mountains.

8 Our lives **were** _____ **in the balance**, but our boat was eventually rescued from the storm.

9 He's **on** _____ to beat the world record if he carries on at this speed.

2 Complete the sentences with a word or phrase in bold from Exercise 1 in the correct form.

1 All our hard work on the project will have _____ if we're awarded the contract.

2 We knew winning it was _____, but we entered the badminton competition after training for just a few weeks.

3 We lost our jobs and had no other options. As we _____, we decided to set up our own business.

4 It's a _____ five-hour race, which not everyone finishes.

5 It's important to be able to _____ and sort out unexpected problems when they occur.

6 Emma's company was losing money, and its survival was _____ until she got a loan from the bank.

7 Louis got _____ when he agreed to help his friend build a boat – he hadn't expected it to take two years!

8 Keep working hard – you're _____ to achieve your ambitions!

9 This blog will warn you about all the common _____ related to making a short film on your phone.

3 Read the article on the opposite page, quickly. Which of the following could be an alternative title?

A Two cyclists plan a trip together
B Two cyclists compare notes
C Two cyclists compete in a race

PREPARE FOR THE EXAM

Reading and Use of English Part 5

4 Read the article again. For questions 1–6, choose the answer (A, B, C or D) which you think fits best according to the text.

1 What do we learn about Buhring in the first paragraph?
   A She preferred to ignore the potential pitfalls she faced.
   B She feels she got more than she had bargained for during her trip.
   C She has no regrets about her decision to start her trip when she did.
   D She takes pride in how quickly she acquired new skills before leaving.

2 What point does the writer make in the second paragraph?
   A He was determined to fully appreciate his adventure.
   B There is nothing particularly special about what he achieved.
   C Some people are unable to rise to the occasion when necessary.
   D It was worth attempting to beat a record because he had nothing to lose.

3 What is the writer doing in the third paragraph?
   A illustrating how much he and Buhring have in common
   B complaining about the gruelling nature of long-distance cycling
   C explaining how he and Buhring coped with various challenges
   D comparing the difficulties of cycling in different parts of the world

4 What does the writer suggest in the fourth paragraph?
   A Both he and Buhring took risks that ultimately paid off.
   B Buhring had a more enjoyable experience than he did.
   C It was easier for Buhring to deal with practicalities than it was for him.
   D Neither he nor Buhring ever found the success of their trips hanging in the balance.

5 What does Buhring say about herself in the final paragraph?
   A She intends to discover new ways of developing physical fitness.
   B She is motivated by the need to prove how extraordinary she is.
   C She refuses to accept that she will have to give up sport one day.
   D She is eager to keep on investigating her own capabilities.

6 In the passage as a whole, what is the writer's attitude to Buhring?
   A He is impressed by her strength of character.
   B He thinks that some of her aims are a long shot.
   C He doubts whether she will ever be completely satisfied.
   D He admires the way in which she has dealt with setbacks.

EXAM TIP

Don't worry if you don't understand every single word or phrase in the text – you should usually still be able to answer the questions.

CYCLING ROUND THE WORLD

Round-the-world cyclist Rob Penn interviews Juliana Buhring.

Juliana Buhring is regarded as one of the world's strongest ultra-endurance adventure cyclists. In 2012, she cycled 29,000 kilometres through 19 countries in just 152 days, setting a Guinness World Record. She had a friend at home in Italy providing logistical support, but most days she set off on her bike, 'Pegasus', carrying only bare essentials, not knowing where she would sleep that night. She averaged 200 kilometres a day. It's a remarkable achievement, particularly for someone who had never really been on a bicycle before she was 30. 'I remember riding a bike with training wheels in a playground as a six-year-old,' she says. 'That was the sum total of my experience until I decided to cycle round the world. I knew next to nothing about bike technology or the science of cycling. I trained for eight months. Then I just felt I was ready. I could have delayed it, to get fitter or secure more funding, but I might never have left. Many people postpone making their dreams a reality to wait for the perfect time. There is no such thing.'

I, too, rode a bicycle around the Earth. I pedalled 25,000 miles through 40 countries in the late 1990s, though my circumnavigation took more than 1,000 days, some seven times longer than Buhring's. You don't need a wealth of knowledge and experience to embark on a journey like this. If you believe that human wisdom may be measured by the respect we pay to the unattainable, the mysterious or simply the different, and you have a flair for getting on with people, then you're ready to leave now. I think the new wave of cyclists who circumnavigate the world merely to set records are missing the point. Why set off on a great journey and then dash furiously towards the end of it? When I left, my intention was to go as slowly as possible.

Inevitably we discuss wind – the master of every long-distance cyclist's morale. Buhring was blown off the road on a volcanic plateau in New Zealand, while I rode straight into the wind for six weeks across Uzbekistan and Turkmenistan. We exchange thoughts on the basic but profound pleasure of satisfying pure hunger, and on our favourite national street cuisines – Thai and Turkish food came out on top. We also reflect on the self-discipline required on a long bicycle journey, on the conflict between intense, momentary experiences and the hours of boredom, on learning to communicate without language, and on the deep, luxurious, dreamless sleep that so often follows a full day's cycling.

Buhring used technology that didn't exist when I was wandering. She listened to audio books, while I taped poems to my handlebars and learned them to make things less tedious. She had a GPS device, while I had paper maps, although we both often navigated by the sun. When her money ran out halfway round, she crowdfunded the rest of the journey, receiving hundreds of small donations from people following her on social media, as well as offers of food and accommodation. When I was broke, I stopped and worked. I ask her if she had a sense of the world being bigger or smaller when she got back. The answer is smaller. Here we differ. I had an overwhelming sense of it being much bigger when I returned after three years. Even now, 17 years later, I often think of the Karakoram Mountains, the red earth of the Australian outback and the deserts of Iran. Thus, I am reminded what an implausibly huge, infinitely varied planet we inhabit.

Since setting the Guinness record, Buhring has become a formidable endurance athlete. 'I'm fascinated by what we can do when we don't imagine we possibly can,' Buhring says. 'I'm curious about our unexplored potential, and this is not just cycling, right? I'm interested in the whole mind and body connection. Most people have a panic alarm that says "Stop!" when the body really hurts, but you might still have 20% of your energy left. How do you get that last 20% out of yourself? My ambition is to push myself a bit harder, to see how far I can go. It's not about rewriting record books. I don't consider myself a unique physical specimen. I have turned myself into an athlete. I'm experimenting. I keep stretching my limits, and I can't be content with anything less than knowing I could not have ridden any harder.'

5 Match the **highlighted** words or phrases in the text to the definitions.

1 raised money online from a large number of people

2 found a direction across, along or over an area of water or land

3 natural ability to do something well

4 obtain

5 in a way that is difficult to believe

GRAMMAR
FRONTING AND INVERSION

1 Choose the correct options.

1 *Not only / No way* are we on track to win the league, but we might win the cup, too.

2 *Hardly / Little* did we know there was a storm coming that would ruin our plans.

3 *Best / Most* of all is that you don't have to take an exam at the end of the course.

4 *Funnier / So funny* than any other comedian that night was my friend Mark.

5 *Little / No way* is Daniel going to agree to do a parachute jump for charity.

6 *Just / Not only* half a kilometre from our hotel was the best restaurant in the city.

7 *So / Most* gruelling was the climb back down the mountain that it took them days to recover.

8 *Two hours later / Not only* they announced that our flight was cancelled.

2 Match the fronting structures 1–8 in Exercise 1 to their descriptions, A–H.

A *so* + adjective ....

B comparative phrase ....

C positive phrase with a limited meaning ....

D negative phrase with a positive meaning ....

E negative phrase meaning something that someone doesn't want to happen ....

F phrase describing location or position ....

G superlative adjective ....

H adverbial phrase of time or place ....

3 Complete the sentences with the words in brackets in the correct order.

0 So *cold was it outside* (outside / cold / it / was) that the penguins were shivering.

1 Not until I got home .... (realise / I / did) I'd left my laptop on the train.

2 Such .... (delight / was / Ana's) at being chosen for the role that she screamed.

3 At no time .... (were / permitted / we) to leave the school without permission.

4 Only when she reached the summit .... (she / did / feel) that she had finally achieved something great.

5 Under no circumstances .... (the door / you / open / should) while the train is in motion.

6 No way .... (am / going to / I / lend) you £500!

4 Complete the blog post with the words in the box.

just   little   never   only   so   until   way   worst

ADVENTURE HOLIDAY   🔍

Not [1] .... was I happy to win a 'mystery' adventure holiday in the Peak District, I was also astonished. I had never won anything in my life before! However, [2] .... did I know what a nightmare was coming my way.

I should have known better. For a start, I am not really an outdoors person. Secondly, I'm not particularly fit. But [3] .... of all, I am afraid of heights – not the ideal characteristic for someone going to spend a weekend – as it turned out – climbing mountains! Unfortunately, not [4] .... the minibus pulled up outside the climbing centre, at the foot of a huge mountain, did I realise the error I had made.

At first, I decided to go along with the rest of my fellow adventurers. [5] .... enthusiastic were they that I thought I might be able to rise to the occasion and join them in the adventure. [6] .... have I been more mistaken.

[7] .... a short walk from the climbing centre was the highest cliff I had ever seen. 'No [8] .... am I going up there,' I said to myself. Then I said the same thing to the instructor. And that was the end of my adventure holiday.

5 Rewrite the sentences using the fronting words and phrases in the box.

Just   Little   No way   Not only   Not until   So

1 I am not going to sell you my ticket.

2 He is disappointed, and he's angry as well.

3 A great pizza place is only five minutes' walk from here.

4 We were unaware that we were going to get more than we bargained for.

5 It was such a dull film that we walked out before it was over.

6 You only realise how much you love something after you lose it.

👁 6 Correct the mistakes in the sentences or put a tick by any you think are correct.

1 Not only the routes are long, but they are also extremely difficult.

2 Never before I climbed such a dangerous cliff. ....

3 No way is she going to agree to such a deal. ....

4 So furious the professor was that he could hardly speak.

5 Little did they know that the success of the project was hanging in the balance. ....

6 At no time I did ever feel in any real danger. ....

VOCABULARY
VERB PHRASES WITH *MAKE, TAKE, HAVE* AND *GET*

1 Choose the correct options.

1 When you obtain something that was not easy to get, you manage to get *your hands on / stock of* it.
2 If something has become impossible to control, it has got *out of hand / a move on.*
3 If you have only one possible choice, you have *no option but / effect* to do it.
4 When you do something consciously and deliberately, you are making *a point / the hang* of doing it.
5 To get *the hang of / your hands on* something, you first need to practise doing it.
6 When you start taking *an interest in / stock of* something, you begin to pay attention to it.
7 People get *a move / their hands* on when they need to hurry up.
8 When you try to change something, but it stays the same, you have *no effect / no option* on it.
9 If someone survives a difficult situation, we can say they have made *it / a point of it.*
10 To take *effect on / stock of* a situation means 'to evaluate it before making a decision'.

2 Complete the sentences, using your answers from Exercise 1 to help you.

1 James has _____ an interest in music and recently bought a piano. He's been practising for a few weeks now, but hasn't quite _____ the hang of it yet.
2 The meeting began to _____ out of hand when some of the people attending were offended by the chairperson's behaviour. Eventually, we _____ no option but to call the police.
3 **A:** Have you managed to _____ your hands on that book you need for your course?
   B: Not yet.
   A: Well, you'd better _____ a move on! You're starting next week.
4 Having _____ stock of our financial situation, I have concluded that our business will be lucky to _____ it through this crisis.
5 The only thing that will _____ a positive effect on your grades this year is if you _____ a point of attending every lecture.

3 Complete the sentences with the correct preposition.

1 I can't wait to get my hands _____ that new computer game.
2 Although he tried, he never got the hang _____ skateboarding.
3 Please get a move _____ – we're already ten minutes late!
4 What was it that made you take an interest _____ the stock market?
5 It is time to take a break and take stock _____ what we have achieved so far.
6 I am afraid we have no option but _____ ask the bank for another loan.

4 Match the sentence halves.

1 If we don't get a move on,
2 Although it was a long shot,
3 We have had no luck getting
4 None of the students took
5 This treatment is having
6 After a year's training, it's time to

a no effect at all – my back still really hurts.
b our hands on tickets for the music festival.
c take stock of how much progress we have made.
d an interest in the free Mandarin lessons on offer.
e the match will have started by the time we arrive.
f we had no option but to try to escape.

1 _____ 3 _____ 5 _____
2 _____ 4 _____ 6 _____

PREPARE FOR THE EXAM

Reading and Use of English Part 2

5 For questions 1–8, read the text below and think of the word which best fits each gap. Use only one word in each gap. There is an example (0) at the beginning.

*How to **change** someone's mind*

A disagreement with a friend can be devastating **(0)** *if* it touches on something important to you both. Maybe you strongly object **(1)** _____ an opinion of theirs which you find offensive, and nothing you say seems to **(2)** _____ an effect on them. What do you do?

It is possible to change someone's mind, but you **(3)** _____ remember that this is not achieved through confrontation. Firstly, make a point **(4)** _____ listening to what your friend has to say. Ask questions and take a genuine interest **(5)** _____ their answers.

A useful technique is to try to express your opponent's position in **(6)** _____ a clear and fair way that they feel reassured that you have listened to them. **(7)** _____ when you have reached this stage should you present them with your counter arguments.

Do not be afraid to end the conversation if emotions begin to get **(8)** _____ of hand. Nothing will close a mind faster than an angry word.

EXAM TIP

Revising phrasal verbs is useful preparation for this part of the exam.

WRITING
AN ESSAY

» SEE *PREPARE TO WRITE* BOX, STUDENT'S BOOK PAGE 79

1 Look at the list of sports and activities below. Which one do you think is the most risky? Which one do you think is the least risky? Why?

1 horse riding
2 rock climbing
3 ice hockey
4 breakdancing
5 canoeing
6 rugby
7 mountain biking

2 Why do you think people enjoy doing leisure activities that involve some risk?

3 Read the task. Think of two activities for each bullet point. Have you done any of these activities? If you have, did you enjoy them? If you haven't, would you like to?

> You have recently heard a discussion about people who do activities in their free time that can involve some risk. You have made the notes below.
>
> **Risk factors for free-time activities:**
> • They are done alone.
> • Participants are often injured.
> • They take place in remote locations.
>
> > **Some opinions expressed in the discussion:**
> > 'People always benefit from strengthening their self-reliance.'
> > 'It's irresponsible to do things that may mean you have to be rescued, with great difficulty, by others.'
> > 'No physical activity is without some degree of risk – even crossing the road can be dangerous.'
>
> Write an essay discussing **two** of the ways in your notes in which free-time activities may involve risk. You should **explain which one of the risk factors is the easiest to justify people taking, giving reasons** to support your opinion.
> You may, if you wish, make use of the opinions expressed in the discussion, but you should use your own words as far as possible.

4 Read the essay by a student called Berta, ignoring the gaps. How many of your activities from Exercise 3 does she discuss? Has she answered the question in full? Is the essay written formally enough?

Many people's idea of a perfect day is ¹ _____ spent curled up on the sofa, binge-watching a detective series. ² _____, however, prefer to do ³ _____ more energetic, like jogging in the park or going to the gym. And then there are those ⁴ _____, not content with ⁵ _____ ordinary activities, go out in search of more adventure.

The ⁶ _____ include sailors and snowboarders, many of ⁷ _____ have chosen their sport ⁸ _____ only because they enjoy it, ⁹ _____ also for the thrill it gives them. The question ¹⁰ _____, are they justified in doing activities that may end up with ¹¹ _____ having to be rescued from rough seas, or spending months in hospital with broken limbs? After all, it's one thing to choose to take a risk ¹² _____, but quite another to put members of the emergency services in danger, or take up a hospital bed, all for the sake of a hobby.

Arguably, snowboarders often practise their sport in groups, so can look after ¹³ _____ other, should an accident occur. Nevertheless, there is always the chance that they may seriously injure ¹⁴ _____. What distinguishes them from sailors, in my view, is the degree of choice they have over the level of risk they take.

Sailors are often miles from land, and weather conditions at sea can change in an instant. If they get into trouble, ¹⁵ _____ frequently results in a great deal of danger for the brave helicopter or boat crews, ¹⁶ _____ job it is to rescue them. I would therefore say, on balance, that it is easier to justify taking physical risks than doing activities in remote places.

5 Complete the essay using one of the options below in each gap. Add capital letters where necessary.

> but   each   is   it   latter   not   one   others
> something   such   them   themselves   who
> whom   whose   yourself

6 Complete the sentences so that each one has the same meaning as the sentence above it, using the word in brackets.

1 Unless people try skateboarding for themselves, they cannot appreciate the skill involved.
It is only ....
.... (that)

2 The most important thing is that people should consider the risk to others.
Above ....
.... (else)

3 The possibility of animal habitats being harmed is of even greater concern.
Of ....
.... (might)

4 Bungee jumping is quite frightening, which is the thing that makes it so appealing.
What ....
.... (fact)

7 Identify the repetition in the sentences below and replace it with a word from the box in the correct form.

> barrier   complicate   ~~demand~~   stimulate
> struggle   overcome

0 The children found making the model robot a real challenge – they almost gave up because it was so <u>challenging</u>.   *demanding*

1 We thought we had finished the difficult project, but then we were told there were some difficulties.
....

2 My cycling trip was far from effortless! Tackling that steep hill was a real effort. ....

3 There was a lot for her to deal with on her journey; for example, she had to deal with her fear of heights before she could cross the mountain bridge. ....

4 An interest many people share is solving puzzles – they find it interesting. ....

5 He faced many obstacles in his life, and one of the biggest obstacles to achieving his goals was his lack of confidence. ....

8 Read the essay question. Plan your essay. Which two challenges are you going to discuss? What might make these things difficult?

> You have recently watched a programme about people who have gone to live in another country and how they dealt with the challenges they encountered. You have made the notes below.
>
> **Aspects of moving to another country which may prove challenging:**
> • maintaining existing relationships
> • acquiring new language skills
> • adapting to a different lifestyle
>
> > **Some opinions expressed in the discussion:**
> > 'Learning new things may keep the brain healthy, but it's time-consuming and difficult.'
> > 'People in different cultures approach things in such very different ways.'
> > 'Keeping in touch with people is never a problem these days.'
>
> Write an essay discussing **two** of the challenges in your notes that people may have to deal with when moving to another country. You should **explain which challenge you think is the greater, giving reasons** to support your opinion.
> You may, if you wish, make use of the opinions expressed in the discussion, but you should use your own words as far as possible.

 PREPARE FOR THE EXAM

Writing Part 1

9 Write your essay, using some of the techniques you have learned to avoid repetition. Write 220–260 words.

✓ **EXAM TIP**

In an essay, although you must give your own opinion, don't write about yourself – write about people in general.

11 JOG YOUR MEMORY

VOCABULARY AND READING
MEMORY AND FORGETTING

1 Complete the missing words in the sentences. The first letter of each word is given.

1 People with memory loss find it very difficult to r_____ individual memories.

2 There are several d_____ between my memory of the event and my sister's. She thought it was much worse than I did.

3 I sometimes have f_____ to the night of the accident, which is why I always get nervous riding my bike on the road.

4 My brother only has v_____ memories of his early childhood. He can't recall most of it, unfortunately.

5 I was supposed to call my friend this morning, but it completely s_____ m_____ m_____. I'll call her tomorrow.

6 The hypnotist claimed he could p_____ false memories in people's minds, but I don't believe it for a second.

7 I don't believe a word of that story – I think it was all totally f_____.

8 I can't recall all the details of the presentation, but I can remember t_____ g_____ of it.

9 It's hard to m_____ s_____ o____ what she told me – it was a really long and complicated story.

10 I don't want to t_____ upsetting memories by asking her about what happened that day.

2 Complete the sentences with completed words or expressions in bold from Exercise 1.

1 Do you think it's possible to _____ a false memory deliberately?

2 I can't remember that day very clearly at all – it's all rather _____.

3 Try and give me _____ of what she said – I don't need all the details.

4 I'm sure he was lying – everything he said sounded completely _____.

5 There are tricks you can learn to help you _____ vocabulary items when you need them.

6 I couldn't _____ the little boy's story – it was hard to understand – but he thought it was funny!

7 War reporters sometimes suffer from _____ to the time they spent in conflict zones.

8 Hearing that song might _____ some unhappy memories for you – I'd skip it.

9 There were no _____ between the two witnesses' stories. They had exactly the same account of the night of the accident.

10 I'm sorry I didn't bring your book back today – it completely _____.

SHOPPING LIST
1.
2.
3.

3 Read the first paragraph of the article on the opposite page. What does Liana say about her earliest memory?

A It is something she remembered again recently.

B It is one of many she has from that time.

C It probably isn't a genuine memory.

 ## PREPARE FOR THE EXAM

Reading and Use of English Part 8

4 You are going to read an article in which four different people talk about memory. For questions 1–10, choose from the people (A–D). The people may be chosen more than once.

Which person

1 expresses doubt about their ability to develop better habits? _____

2 shows enthusiasm for becoming involved in an area of study? _____

3 mentions differences between the types of things that people recall? _____

4 says the general idea of taking responsibility for improving one's own memory is appealing? _____

5 acknowledges that a theory about early memories is likely to be correct? _____

6 describes the impact of frequently talking about the past? _____

7 regrets failing to follow useful advice? _____

8 admits to having taken pride in their powers of recall? _____

9 explains why people are motivated to repeat a particular activity? _____

10 offers a reason why some early memories are lost? _____

EXAM TIP

The words in the question are very unlikely to appear in the part of the text which matches the idea.

5 Match the highlighted words or phrases in the text to the definitions.

1 feeling of being embarrassed _____

2 remembered for a long time _____

3 changing and correcting _____

4 understand something by collecting different bits of information _____

5 changing things completely for the better _____

Memory

A Liana

I'd always been convinced I could remember playing with another child and falling over and hurting myself when I was about one year old, but I've recently read that this kind of early memory is probably fabricated. Apparently, research suggests that it isn't possible to have a memory from earlier than the age of two, and I'm prepared to believe that – if a little reluctantly. Though I do have what feel like flashbacks to that moment, I can accept that I may be creating a false memory, possibly from family photographs. It's a bit disappointing because, I must confess, I'd always felt rather pleased with myself for being able to remember my early childhood like that. I suppose we piece things together from various sources, and thinking they're memories is one way of making sense of all that information. Research into memory is a fascinating field, I think, and I'd love to discover more about it. You never know – maybe I'll even get to do some myself one day.

B Mesul

Thinking of the brain as a muscle is so constructive because it means there are actually things I can do myself to enhance my capacity to memorise things effectively. That would help me with my studies because I tend to forget things rather quickly, and sometimes find it hard to retrieve facts and figures when I need them. It turns out that it's not only memory games that are really helpful, whether played alone or with others, but also crosswords and jigsaw puzzles. Doing jigsaws without looking at the picture on the box is supposed to train your short-term memory, too. Sorting out all the colours and shapes to put the picture together provides a great mental workout, apparently, and every time you fit two pieces together correctly, the brain gets a shot of dopamine – a chemical that triggers feelings of happiness – thus encouraging you to try the experience again. There are also plenty of memory apps that do the same for your brain, making it pleasurable to develop your abilities.

C Raine

Did you know that as little as an hour after reading something, most people have forgotten more than half of it? There's a technique called *spaced repetition* that is said to help. By reviewing what you've learned at regular intervals, you can hold on to the information for a longer period of time. My teachers recommend this approach, and I can see it makes sense, but to my shame, I've so far lacked the strength of character to do it. I'm one of those people who always ends up revising things at the last minute. If I'm asked a couple of days later about what I learned, I find it virtually impossible to say anything relevant about it, although I may retain some of the gist, if I'm lucky. I accept that there are ways of rectifying this, which I'm prepared to try, but, deep down, I wonder if I'll ever succeed in turning things around.

D Hugo

I'm interested in the links between language and memory. According to one study, children who are able to speak at the time of a particular event are able to remember that event for up to five years later. In contrast, children who have not yet started speaking at the time of an incident only have very vague memories of it, if they can remember it at all. This seems to suggest that unless a memory can be translated into language, it isn't retained. Furthermore, in societies where children are regularly encouraged to share memories about important events in their lives, they learn to structure these memories so that they can communicate them effectively. Creating these family stories makes the events easier to remember later in life. Moreover, in societies where parents focus more on memories of children's individual experiences, children are more likely to remember personal achievements, while children in other societies may remember more about they did with groups of their peers.

GRAMMAR
PASSIVE REVIEW

1 Choose the correct options.

1 Many memories of my childhood *were / have been* triggered when I returned to my old school.
2 The suspect's story is now believed *to be / being* completely fabricated.
3 I got *bit / bitten* by a spider when I was on holiday in Australia.
4 Mark is very unhappy about *to be / being* paid so little for his work.
5 We regret to inform you that flight BA321 *was / has been* delayed for three hours.
6 It is important that you follow the rules in order to avoid *to be / being* penalised.

2 Match the structures A–F to the sentences 1–6 in Exercise 1.

A passive gerund (with *be*) ....
B passive gerund (after a preposition) ....
C passive infinitive (with *to*) ....
D past participle (with *get*) ....
E past simple passive (with *be*) ....
F present perfect passive ....

3 Rewrite the sentences, using the underlined verb in the passive.

1 He said that nobody <u>told</u> him anything about the deal.
   He denied ....
2 Take the GPS device, or you might <u>lose</u> your way.
   Take the GPS device, ...
3 They <u>planted</u> a false memory in his mind.
   A false memory ....
4 I do not give you permission to <u>experiment</u> on me.
   I do not agree ....
5 'Do not let anyone <u>mislead</u> you,' he advised us.
   He warned us ....
6 We have <u>noticed</u> a discrepancy.
   A discrepancy ....

CAUSATIVES

4 Complete the sentences using the verbs in the box in the correct form.

> behave   break   complain   deliver   do   fix
> hand in   stay   take

1 Daniel had his nose .... during a rugby match.
2 If you want the job done properly, get a professional
   .... it.
3 I'm not having you .... up all night on the computer
   and then .... about how tired you are tomorrow.
4 I had my motorbike .... last week.
5 Why don't we phone a restaurant and have them
   .... some food?
6 'I want those essays .... on Friday morning,' said
   the lecturer.
7 I won't have my students .... in that disrespectful
   way.
8 The athlete had his medal .... away from him
   when it was discovered that he had cheated.

5 Complete the sentences using the words in brackets in a causative or passive structure.

0 They've arranged for *the flat to be cleaned* (the flat / clean) tomorrow afternoon.
1 Let's .... (a taxi / pick) us up
   after the party.
2 I'm tired of .... (choose) last for every
   team game. It makes me feel so unwanted.
3 Our car's .... (tyres / let down)
   while it was parked in the driveway. Who would do such
   a thing?
4 Shall we .... (dinner / deliver)
   to the flat this evening?
5 The teacher wants .... (this
   project / finish) by Monday next week.
6 I .... (my dad / repair) my
   broken scooter.

⊙ 6 Correct the mistakes in the sentences or put a tick by any you think are correct.

1 I'd appreciate to be informed of any change in the
   schedule. ....
2 You should get your eyes examining. ....
3 Unfortunately, *History Today* magazine doesn't be
   distributed any more. ....
4 No experiments were carried out yet. ....
5 Why don't you get someone change your tyre for you?
   ....
6 I'm not having that man talk to me like that again. ....

7 Write sentences that are true for you using passive and causative structures.

1 An event that triggered memories for you
   Memories of ....
   ....
2 If you had a robot that could do anything, what would
   you have it do for you?
   If ....
   ....
3 When something unwanted happened to you
   I ....
   ....
4 Something that somebody taught you which you have
   never forgotten
   I have ....
   ....

VOCABULARY
PREFIXES

1 Add the prefixes to the words and then match them to the definitions.

> out-   over-   re-   under-

1 _____ charged
2 _____ cooked
3 _____ consider
4 _____ dated
5 _____ do
6 _____ grown
7 _____ qualified
8 _____ staffed

a think about something again
b having more skills, knowledge or experience than necessary
c when food is not heated for sufficient time
d too old or mature for something
e perform an action again
f not having enough people working in a place
g asked to pay too much money for something
h old-fashioned

1 _____   3 _____   5 _____   7 _____
2 _____   4 _____   6 _____   8 _____

2 Complete the sentences by adding a prefix from Exercise 1 to the words in the box.

> apply   grow   introduce
> paid   protective   sell

1 If you are not accepted onto the training programme this year, you are welcome to _____ next year.
2 Printed books still _____ e-books by around 80%.
3 Most student summer jobs are seriously _____. Students don't make much money at all from them.
4 Some environmentalists have been campaigning to _____ wolves and bears into their natural habitats.
5 I hope I don't become one of those _____ parents who don't let their children do anything exciting.
6 What present do you buy for a child who has _____ toys?

NEGATIVE PREFIXES

3 Make the words in the table negative by adding a prefix from the box.

> dis-   in-   mis- (x2)   un-

positive	negative
considerate	1 _____
lead	2 _____
professional	3 _____
respectful	4 _____
understanding	5 _____

4 Complete the conversations with the words from Exercise 3 in the correct form.

1 **A:** That sign in your shop window is _____. It says there's a sale, but everything costs the same as before!
 B: I'm sorry for the _____. The sale is over. I forgot to take the sign down.
2 **A:** Excuse me. Why have you parked your car on the pavement? It's very _____ – people are trying to get past.
 B: I'm on my lunch break.
 A: The fact that you're a driving instructor makes it _____, too. Is this what you teach your students?
 B: Go away, you're boring me.
 A: Don't be so _____! I'm going to report you.

PREPARE FOR THE EXAM

Reading and Use of English Part 3

5 For questions 1–8, read the text below. Use the word given in capitals at the end of some of the lines to form a word that fits in the gap in the same line. There is an example at the beginning (0).

Why I am an archaeologist

As an archaeologist, I am often asked what it was that **(0)** _originally_ attracted me to the profession. I must confess that it was the Indiana Jones series of films that were my **(1)** _____. Of course, those films gave a very **(2)** _____ impression of the life of an archaeologist. Jones is a **(3)** _____ character created for our entertainment, and it must be recognised that he behaved extremely **(4)** _____ at times. That was part of the attraction!

I have since **(5)** _____ my desire to copy that heroic adventurer with his leather hat and whip, but I do not regret my decision to become an archaeologist. It was hard at first. Entry-level positions are still very **(6)** _____. But, eventually, I got a job on a government team as a **(7)** _____. If there are plans to build a road or shopping centre somewhere, we go in first to make sure there are no sites of archaeological interest that might be affected. Also, construction of projects sometimes risk disturbing ancient burial sites, and it's important to avoid being **(8)** _____ in such cases.

ORIGIN

INSPIRE
LEAD

FICTION

PROFESSION

GROW

PAY

CONSULT

RESPECT

EXAM TIP

Make sure you spell the words correctly. You will not get a mark if the right word is wrongly spelled.

1 Look at the photo below. What are the people doing? Would you like to do it? Why? / Why not?

....
....
....
....

2 Read all of the questions in Exercise 6. What part of speech is required in each gap?

1 ....   5 ....
2 ....   6 ....
3 ....   7 ....
4 ....   8 ....

3 Look again at the questions in Exercise 6 and try to guess what word will fit in each gap.

1 ....   5 ....
2 ....   6 ....
3 ....   7 ....
4 ....   8 ....

4 Which sentence in Exercise 6 will be completed with the following?

A something an archaeologist might find ....
B a kind of book or database ....
C a type of container ....
D a subject/hobby/fascination ....
E a form of accommodation ....
F a therapeutic activity ....

5 The sentences that do not appear in the answers for Exercise 4 are more 'open'. What kind of things could fit?

....
....

 PREPARE FOR THE EXAM

Listening Part 2

 6 You'll hear part of a careers talk by an archaeologist called Sandra Liggins. For questions 1–8, complete the sentence with a word or short phrase.

1 Sandra says it was her interest in .... which led her to study archaeology.
2 Sandra explains that to get a place on an archaeological dig as a volunteer, a .... is usually required.
3 Sandra chose to stay in a .... when she went on her first dig.
4 Significant finds are placed in a .... for further inspection.
5 Every object that is found is recorded in something called a .... first of all.
6 Sandra says that a .... was the item that she was most happy to find on her first day.
7 Sandra believes that a regular .... helps keep her and her diggers healthy.
8 Sandra reveals that .... are not generally popular among archaeologists.

 EXAM TIP

All the answers are actual words you hear in the recording. You must spell the words correctly.

READING AND USE OF ENGLISH

1 Part 1 of the *Reading and Use of English* exam often tests your knowledge of idiomatic phrases. Complete the idiomatic phrases below.

1 I don't like him – he _____ me up the wrong way.
   A puts   **B** rubs   **C** wipes   **D** combs

2 We never _____ eye to eye on anything.
   A look   **B** watch   **C** see   **D** agree

2 Look at the gaps in Exercise 3. Four of them are idioms. Can you identify them?

_____

✓ PREPARE FOR THE EXAM

Reading and Use of English Part 1

3 Read the text below and decide which answer (A, B, C or D) best fits each gap. There is an example at the beginning (0).

Your Memory Mind Palace

Everybody's memory lets them **(0)** *down* from time to time. Important things **(1)** _____ your mind. Fortunately, it is quite easy to **(2)** _____ improve your memory by learning a simple technique – *the mind palace*. Why not give it a try? You've got **(3)** _____ to lose!

Let's **(4)** _____ you have to remember a list of things. First, you need to think of a place you know **(5)** _____ out, like your own house. In your imagination, starting at your front door, go through the house, **(6)** _____ places where you can put things: the doormat, the table in the kitchen, etc.

The idea is to **(7)** _____ the things on your list with those places in your mind palace in amusing ways. If the first two things on your list are bread and milk, imagine your doormat is a huge slice of bread and a cow is sitting on the table. Do that for everything on your list. You won't forget anything – but you might not be able to walk round the supermarket with a **(8)** _____ face.

0 A out	**B** down	**C** off	**D** up
1 A miss	**B** lose	**C** slip	**D** drop
2 A radically	**B** extremely	**C** totally	**D** absolutely
3 A zero	**B** nothing	**C** anything	**D** none
4 A think	**B** tell	**C** say	**D** state
5 A all	**B** outside	**C** through	**D** inside
6 A identifying	**B** pointing	**C** discovering	**D** indicating
7 A equate	**B** associate	**C** mix	**D** attach
8 A right	**B** blank	**C** square	**D** straight

✓ EXAM TIP

Read the title and the text quickly to get an understanding of what it is about.

4 Read the article in Exercise 7 quickly. Does the writer think it is possible to travel through time?

_____

5 Look at the example (0). Write as many forms of the word *inspire* as you can. Include opposites. Why is *inspiration* the only correct answer in the text?

_____
_____

6 Look at gaps 1–8 in Exercise 7. What part of speech is required in each one?

1 _____	4 _____	7 _____
2 _____	5 _____	8 _____
3 _____	6 _____	

✓ PREPARE FOR THE EXAM

Reading and Use of English Part 3

7 For questions 1–8, read the text below. Use the word given in capitals at the end of some of the lines to form a word that fits in the gap in the same line. There is an example at the beginning (0).

TIME TRAVEL

The idea of time travel has been the **(0)** *inspiration* for thousands of sci-fi stories. But is it possible? The simple answer is yes. In fact, we all travel **(1)** _____ through time every day, at the speed of one second per second.
(2) _____ may make you feel like you are travelling too slowly, but the future will always arrive.

We can also look *back* in time with NASA's **(3)** _____ telescopes, which point at distant galaxies. The light from those galaxies takes millions of years to reach Earth. As a **(4)** _____, we are seeing what they looked like millions of years ago.

According to Einstein's theory, it is also possible to travel forward in time. However, it would involve moving at an **(5)** _____ speed to travel any meaningful distance into the future.
Travelling backwards in time, although **(6)** _____ a possibility, is much harder. But the idea of going into the past in order to change something in the present is **(7)** _____ impossible, and based on a **(8)** _____ of the laws of physics.

INSPIRE

EFFORT

PATIENT

ASTRONOMY

CONSEQUENT

IMAGINE

REPUTE

LOGIC
UNDERSTAND

✓ EXAM TIP

Always read the text again when you have finished to check that it makes sense.

12 CHANGING TIMES

VOCABULARY AND READING
SOCIAL CHANGE

1 Complete the sentences with the words in the box.

> affluent   disposable   ends   gap   laid   means
> outgoings   overcrowding   reformed   tackle
> tighten   unaffordable

1 What's your _____ income at the moment?
2 If the taxation system is _____, it might become fairer.
3 Many very _____ people live in this expensive part of town.
4 Cars were largely _____ for my great-grandparents' generation.
5 They're trying to _____ the problem of large companies not paying their taxes.
6 Many people where I live don't have the _____ to pay their rent.
7 When you're on a low income, it's hard to make _____ meet.
8 You'll have to _____ your belt if you accept a job that's lower paid than the one you have now.
9 If your _____ are greater than your income, you're in trouble.
10 The pay _____ between men and women in my workplace is shocking.
11 When the business was doing badly, many employees were _____ off.
12 There's a risk of serious _____ in these flats – the council should build more housing in this area.

2 Match the sentence halves.

1 The gender pay gap is greater
2 She hasn't got the means
3 The overcrowding in this area
4 My disposable income will be reduced
5 I don't know how he makes ends
6 After she was laid off,
7 Since the government's housing policy was reformed,
8 I've tightened my
9 Unemployment is a challenging issue
10 This flat will be unaffordable for her
11 Her parents weren't affluent,
12 My outgoings aren't very high

a it took her several months to find a new job.
b has got worse over the last few years.
c unless she gets a pay rise.
d for any government to tackle.
e in some countries than others.
f belt since I lost my job.
g if my electricity bills go up.
h because I don't spend much on clothes or expensive food.
i meet without help from his family.
j more accommodation has become available in inner-city areas.
k to buy everything she'd like to.
l but she still had a very happy childhood.

1	3	5	7	9	11
2	4	6	8	10	12

3 Complete the sentences so they are true for you.

1 _____ is unaffordable for me.
2 The most affluent area where I live is _____.
3 If I had to tighten my belt, I would _____.
4 The most important problem to tackle in my country is _____.

4 Read what expert A says in the article on the opposite page quickly. Does the expert think that a universal basic income is a good idea?

_____

5 Read the questions in Exercise 8 and underline the key idea in each one.

6 Read what expert A says again. Which key idea from Exercise 8 do they express no opinion about?

_____

7 Highlight the sections in text A that relate to each underlined key idea in the questions in Exercise 8.

 PREPARE FOR THE EXAM

Reading and Use of English Part 6

8 You are going to read four extracts from articles in which experts discuss the idea of a universal basic income. For questions 1–4, choose from the experts A–D. The experts may be chosen more than once.

Which expert

1 shares an opinion with D regarding how the universal basic income should be funded? _____
2 has a different opinion from all the others on who ought to receive the universal basic income? _____
3 holds a similar opinion to A on how easy it would be to implement a universal basic income? _____
4 has a different view from B about how a universal basic income would affect people's motivation to work? _____

 EXAM TIP

In the texts, look for synonyms of key words from the questions. These should help you to find the opinions you are looking for.

UNIVERSAL BASIC INCOME
Four experts give their views

A The idea of a universal basic income is to give people a minimum income – one which is guaranteed by the government. In my view, if such a policy were to be implemented, it should take the form of a monthly payment for all citizens, regardless of their wealth and whether they are in work or not. I would argue in favour of it being financed through the taxation of the most affluent individuals in the country. Such a scheme should be simple to run, as giving a basic income to all would involve a minimum of bureaucracy. As a result, it would cost the government far less than the current schemes designed to tackle poverty. It would be a welcome step towards reducing social inequality in the country as a whole – a highly desirable goal – and provide those who currently struggle to make ends meet with the means to afford a more fulfilling and enjoyable lifestyle.

B Many people believe that a universal basic income is unaffordable for national governments. However, they would be more likely to support this sensible proposal if the money for it were to come from taxing large technology companies at higher rates. Everyone in the country could then be paid a fixed sum each month, enough to cover basic outgoings and provide a reasonable standard of living. Although it might well require complex processes to set up and administer, this should not be beyond our capabilities as a modern high-tech society. Providing a universal basic income might, of course, lead some people to start regarding having a career as optional. There is probably no way of preventing this. Nevertheless, the benefits to the economy coming from every member of society having a disposable income (more money spent, leading to more jobs generated) should not be underestimated. Nor should those of having a more psychologically and physically healthy population.

C Inevitably, a universal basic income would result in fewer people feeling the need to participate in the labour force at any one time. And yet, this wouldn't necessarily be a wholly negative outcome, as it would allow people to care for young children and the elderly at home, or take courses to increase their future employment prospects. On a practical level, a universal basic income should not be hard to introduce and should also be straightforward to manage. It would be preferable, I believe, to only offer it to those who would otherwise fall into poverty. It cannot be wise for a government to support those who already have more than enough to live on. But removing the fear and stress associated with being laid off would certainly improve the well-being of the nation. Some may argue that such a scheme would be too expensive, though making large enterprises pay their fair share would more than cover the cost.

D If our welfare system were to be reformed, or, in fact, replaced altogether by a universal basic income, society as a whole would benefit. I realise that this would involve time and effort, but it would give those in employment more security, and is unlikely to produce a significant increase in unemployment. After all, most adults prefer to be busy and occupied rather than sitting at home doing nothing. Arguably, a universal basic income needs to be a guaranteed income available to each person in the country, with no exceptions. This is the only way to promote equality and improve the lives of the entire population. Currently, a tiny percentage of this country's population owns a major proportion of our national wealth. If these people were made to contribute what they should to the state, it would provide the resources needed several times over.

9 Match the **highlighted words or phrases** in the text to the definitions.

1 the people in a country who are working ....
2 providing a sense of satisfaction ....
3 complicated rules and processes that make it hard to get something done ....
4 without taking into account ....
5 the correct amount ....

GRAMMAR
MODAL PASSIVES

1 Match the modal passive structures in sentences 1–9 to the functions a–i.

1 The car **can't have been repaired** properly because it's still not working.
2 Hundreds of employees **had to be laid off** during the last recession.
3 Greater income equality **can be achieved** with appropriate legislation.
4 We **should have been told** about these financial reforms, but we weren't.
5 Solving the problem of child poverty **should be placed** at the top of the government's agenda.
6 **Could we please be kept** up to date on the latest developments?
7 Anyone finishing early **is allowed to leave** the building.
8 No alterations **can be carried out** without official authorisation.
9 Luckily, my leg **didn't have to be operated on** because the injury wasn't that severe.

a possibility ....
b deduction ....
c prohibition ....
d permission ....
e obligation ....
f lack of obligation ....
g recommendation ....
h regret/criticism ....
i request ....

2 Match the sentence halves.

1 Your outgoings should
2 Can I be given some extra time
3 The demonstration must have
4 This government ought to have
5 All evidence must
6 You're lucky your train was delayed – you might
7 Children must not
8 I don't need to

a be left unattended in the play area.
b be reduced by about 20%.
c been cancelled because there's nobody here.
d to complete my application?
e have missed it.
f be told what to do with my disposable income!
g been voted out at the last election.
h be presented to the court.

1 .... 3 .... 5 .... 7 ....
2 .... 4 .... 6 .... 8 ....

3 What are the functions of the complete sentences in Exercise 2? Use the list of functions in Exercise 1 to help you.

1 .... 5 ....
2 .... 6 ....
3 .... 7 ....
4 .... 8 ....

4 Complete the sentences using the verbs in brackets in the correct form.

1 I'm not sure, but I think we might .... (give) the wrong directions.
2 The amount of crime in this city must .... (reduce) if its citizens are to feel safe.
3 We believe that the law regarding immigration should .... (reform) years ago.
4 I definitely locked my bike up here, and now it's gone – it must .... (steal)!
5 Marco shouldn't .... (invite) to the party next week – he'll just argue with everybody, as usual.
6 The criminal can't .... (arrest) yet because the police say they're still looking for him.
7 Sacrifices don't have to .... (made) if you are affluent and have lots of money.
8 The management must not .... (allow) to lay off any of the workforce.

5 Rewrite the sentences using the passive form.

1 It is possible that nobody saw this sign.
This sign ....
2 You have to pay the bill immediately.
The bill ....
3 It's important that nobody forgets this moment.
This moment ....
4 They should cancel the demonstration.
The demonstration ....
5 I'm certain that nobody had closed the door properly.
The door ....
6 You can see the stadium from my window.
The stadium ....

6 Correct the mistakes in the sentences or put a tick by any you think are correct.

1 You can be asked to show some identification, so take some with you. ....
2 Everyone should paid a basic income by the state, regardless of their wealth. ....
3 The pay gap is something that must to be tackled soon. ....
4 The less affluent shouldn't be told to tighten their belts – they should be helped. ....
5 Education was to be reformed if we're going to eradicate inequality. ....
6 Will you send someone to our room so that our shower could be fixed? ....

VOCABULARY
SYNONYMS AND ANTONYMS

1 Match the words to the definitions.

1	manufacturing	a	buildings for people to live in
2	income	b	money that you receive from working
3	shortage	c	without work
4	diversify	d	the business of producing goods in large quantities
5	jobless		
6	deprivation	e	the legal right to vote
7	suffrage	f	make something more varied
8	housing	g	the state of not having things or conditions usually considered necessary for a pleasant life
		h	when there is not enough of something

1	....	3	....	5	....	7	....
2	....	4	....	6	....	8	....

2 Match the words in Exercise 1 to their synonyms.

1 vary ....
2 unemployed ....
3 right to vote ....
4 salary ....
5 poverty ....
6 industry ....
7 accommodation ....
8 scarcity ....

3 Choose the correct options.

1 The type of product made by the company didn't *vary / diversify* much until the management deliberately began to *vary / diversify*.
2 The word *jobless / unemployed* is less formal than the word *jobless / unemployed*.
3 Women's *suffrage / right to vote* was not universal for much of the 20th century, but today women have the *suffrage / right to vote* in every democratic country.
4 My mother's *salary / income* is only part of our family's combined *salary / income*.
5 The word *poverty / deprivation* refers to economic difficulties, whereas *poverty / deprivation* also refers to other areas which are lacking in something.
6 *Manufacturing / Industry* is just one kind of *manufacturing / industry*.
7 *Accommodation / Housing* often refers to a temporary place to stay, whereas *accommodation / housing* is used for permanent living arrangements.
8 The word *scarcity / shortage* suggests that the lack of something is temporary, whereas *scarcity / shortage* suggests it is more long term.

4 Match the words to the antonyms in the box.

discrimination	expenditure	individual	plentiful
prosperous	rural	weak	wealth

1 deprived ....
2 urban ....
3 fairness ....
4 income ....
5 powerful ....
6 communal ....
7 poverty ....
8 scarce ....

5 Choose the correct options to complete the sentences.

1 We moved from the countryside to the city because we find .... life more exciting.
   A rural   B urban   C individual
2 If your .... exceeds your income, you will eventually have financial difficulties.
   A salary   B wealth   C expenditure
3 We make sure all our employees are treated with .... and respect.
   A fairness   B discrimination   C diversity
4 The leaders of industry are some of the most .... people in the country.
   A plentiful   B weak   C powerful

 PREPARE FOR THE EXAM

Reading and Use of English Part 1

6 Read the text below and decide which answer (A, B, C or D) best fits each gap. There is an example at the beginning (0).

Factfulness – why things are better than we think

When you are watching world news, sometimes it is hard to look on the **(0)** *bright* side. However, according to the **(1)** .... physician and author Hans Rosling, reasons to be optimistic are not as **(2)** .... as you might think. In fact, as he explains in his book *Factfulness*, they are **(3)** ....

The problem, according to Rosling, is partly **(4)** .... to journalists, who constantly seek out sensational stories. Disasters are what generate clicks on social media, and clicks bring in the advertising **(5)** .... for news publishers. Unfortunately, this means that what Rosling calls *the silent miracle of human progress* is overlooked.

The book is full of facts. For example, in the last 20 years, the proportion of the world's population living in **(6)** .... has halved. Also, the number of democratic nations has doubled since 1980, with women having the **(7)** .... to vote in every one of them.

Rosling does not deny there are many problems remaining. Standards of living **(8)** .... from country to country. But he insists that things can be both bad and better at the same time.

0 A shiny	**B** bright	**C** light	**D** white
1 A past	**B** gone	**C** died	**D** late
2 A scarce	**B** thin	**C** short	**D** weak
3 A vast	**B** immense	**C** powerful	**D** plentiful
4 A up	**B** down	**C** over	**D** round
5 A salary	**B** pay	**C** wage	**D** income
6 A poverty	**B** necessity	**C** shortage	**D** deficiency
7 A means	**B** duty	**C** right	**D** suffrage
8 A diversify	**B** vary	**C** change	**D** range

EXAM TIP

If you are not sure of the correct answer, always take a guess.

WRITING
A PROPOSAL

≫ SEE *PREPARE TO WRITE* BOX, STUDENT'S BOOK PAGE 93

1 Make a list of the facilities you think should be provided in a public park.

....

....

....

2 Which four are the most important, in your opinion?

....

....

3 Read the task. What are the points you have to address?

> In the town where you live, there is a large area of land that has not been used for ten years. You believe that a public park should be created on this land. You decide to write a proposal for the town council, explaining why the land should be used in this way, suggesting what kind of things the park could have in it and saying how the park would benefit local people.
> Write your **proposal**.

....

....

....

4 Look at the headings from a sample answer to the question. Decide which paragraph (A–E) should go under each heading. Ignore the gaps in the paragraphs.

Introduction

1 ....

Reasons for using the land for a park

2 ....

What the park might contain

3 ....

Benefits for the local community

4 ....

Conclusion

5 ....

(A) The area is large enough to accommodate gardens for people to relax in and even a small artificial lake. Facilities could include a children's playground, an outdoor café, open areas of grass for games such as football, as well as a basketball court and tennis courts.

(B) 1 ...., all our lives would be enhanced. I would therefore urge the council to give this proposal serious consideration.

(C) Much of the land between the river and the main road into town has been unused for the past ten years. This proposal 2 .... the reasons why a public park should be established there, suggests what the park might be like and explains the 3 .... of the park for local people.

(D) 4 .... that, in order for people in towns and cities to thrive, access to pleasant open spaces close to their homes is essential. This proposal covers the needs of citizens of all ages, and a park would offer them a valuable opportunity to socialise and exercise.

(E) Leaving this large area of land unused in an urban setting 5 .... it becoming an eyesore; rubbish, such as old household appliances, has been discarded there and 6 .... people no longer wanting to walk along that section of the river. 7 .... allowing this situation to persist? 8 .... to transform the area into an attractive and agreeable place, namely a public park.

5 Complete the sample answer in Exercise 4 with the options in the box. Add capital letters where necessary.

> has resulted in   how can the council possibly justify
> numerous studies have shown   one remedy would be
> potential benefits   sets out   this has led to
> were these plans to go ahead

6 Find words in Exercise 4 that mean the following.

> **PARAGRAPH B**
> made much better ....
> strongly encourage ....
>
> **PARAGRAPH D**
> grow, develop or be successful ....
> absolutely necessary ....
> very important ....
>
> **PARAGRAPH E**
> something extremely ugly ....
> continue to exist ....
> completely change ....

7 Complete the sentences with the expressions in the box. Use capital letters where necessary.

> according to   another solution would be   as a result
> is it really worth   research proves that
> this will mean   we can overcome this   we can solve
> what would happen

1 Although there is some resistance to the proposed changes, ... by holding public meetings to discuss them.
2 .... recent research, air quality in the local area is deteriorating rapidly.
3 .... if you continued to ignore the public's concerns?
4 .... these plants absorb large amounts of carbon dioxide.
5 If the area continues to be neglected, ... that it will become more and more unpleasant.
6 I believe that .... this by collaborating with local community groups.
7 In that instance, the council worked very effectively, and .... , everyone was delighted.
8 If offering people discounts for sports equipment doesn't work, ... to offer free coaching.
9 .... risking everything we have worked so hard for at this late stage?

8 Read the task and plan your proposal. How many paragraphs will you write? What could be your heading for each section?

> You have seen an online advertisement from the town council asking for ideas on how to make the high street in your local area more attractive for residents and visitors. You decide to write a proposal for the town council, explaining what could be improved in the high street and suggesting ways of making it a more attractive place to spend time in.
> Write your **proposal**.

PREPARE FOR THE EXAM

Writing Part 2

9 Write your proposal. Use some of the expressions you have learned to make your proposal as persuasive as possible. Write 220–260 words.

✓ EXAM TIP

When writing a proposal, use headings for each paragraph.

VOCABULARY AND READING

THE HONEST TRUTH?

1 Choose the correct options.

1 The email asking for my bank details was a *scam / fraudster*, but I wasn't *fallen for / taken in*.
2 Some people deliberately put *fake / hoax* news on the internet to trick people into believing it.
3 Don't *take in / fall for* that old card trick – you could lose a lot of money.
4 All his stories were so *plausible / far-fetched*, it was impossible to believe them.
5 Sometimes, comedians make *hoax / far-fetched* calls to famous people and record them.
6 The man who tried to fool me was *credibility / supposedly* a friend of my sister's, but in fact, she'd never heard of him.
7 The jury did not believe the witness because her story had no *credibility / hoax*.
8 The children *concocted / fell for* a story to explain the broken window, but their parents weren't fooled.
9 Even though some of the claims in the article are *fake / plausible*, I don't believe them all.

2 Match the definitions to the answers from Exercise 1. One definition matches two answers.

1 made up, invented ....
2 believe a story that is not true ....
3 something designed to trick or deceive people ....
4 fooled by ....
5 according to what someone told you, or according to what is believed by many people to be true ....
6 not true, or not what it is pretending to be ....
7 likely to be possible or true ....
8 the possibility of being believed or trusted ....
9 too unlikely to be believable ....

3 Read the first three paragraphs of the article on the opposite page, ignoring the gaps. Which of the following sentences is true, according to the text?

A All Fools' Day always takes place on April 1st.
B The first day of the Persian New Year is marked with tricks.
C New Year's Day was moved to a different date in Europe in the 16th century.

 PREPARE FOR THE EXAM

Reading and Use of English Part 3

4 Read the first three paragraphs again. For questions 1–8, use the word given in capitals at the end of some of the lines to form a word that fits in the gap in the same line. There is an example (0) at the beginning.

 EXAM TIP

If you have to fill the gap with a noun, check carefully whether it should be singular or plural.

5 Read the rest of the article and answer the questions. Write *Alicia*, *Mark* or *Sam*.

Which person
1 was not fully alert when a trick was played? ....
2 describes carefully selecting who to play a trick on? ....
3 suggests that an idea might be rather good? ....
4 was not particularly amused by an experience? ....
5 wanted to avoid hurting someone's feelings? ....
6 says that a bad habit turned out to be unexpectedly helpful? ....
7 admits that only the timing of something made it seem suspicious? ....
8 fell for a trick despite having been warned in advance? ....

6 Match the highlighted words or phrases in the text to the definitions.

1 what corresponded to ....
2 without a clear mind ....
3 dismiss as untrue ....
4 determine what is correct ....
5 create an even more difficult situation ....

April Fools' Day

A pril Fools' Day is a time for friendly tricks and **(0)** _laughter_ in many countries. Mostly, but not **(1)** _____, celebrated on April 1st, there are several theories about its origin, making it hard to establish the truth with any **(2)** _____ .

Many **(3)** _____ believe that in Europe, it stems from the adoption of the Gregorian calendar in the late 1500s. New Year celebrations were moved from the final week of March to January 1st, and there are **(4)** _____ dating from that time to opponents of the changes being called 'fools' if they were **(5)** _____ to acknowledge the new date.

(6) _____ , in some places, the tradition is far older. In Iran, the 13th day of the Persian New Year usually falls at the beginning of April, and there is evidence that tricks have been played on this day since 536 BCE. More recently, in 1828, a **(7)** _____ publication made April 1st popular in Brazil by producing its first fake headline, **(8)** _____ taking in its readership on that date.

LAUGH
UNIVERSE
CERTAIN
HISTORY

REFER
WILL
NEVER

HUMOUR
SUCCEED

We asked three of our reporters to visit different countries around the time of their version of April Fools' Day last year, and tell us about their experiences.

Alicia in Portugal

When I went to the capital, Lisbon, for the equivalent of April Fools' Day, I knew I should expect practical jokes and hoaxes, but it still felt quite alarming when a bag of flour was thrown all over me by a group of young Portuguese people I'd begun to see as friends. They thought it was hilarious, of course. I wish I could say the same! And to make matters worse, this tradition isn't restricted to a single day, but goes on for two! The one good thing was that, as always, I'd packed several changes of clothes. On most trips, I never wear them all, and feel a bit silly for bringing too much, but this time they were all required! I was into it myself by the end of my stay – it was actually quite thrilling to run through the streets looking for unsuspecting victims, though we only picked people our own age, of course. I'll do more research before taking on an assignment like that again, though.

Mark in Greece

Before I went to Athens for April Fools' Day, I was told that people might concoct stories that were untrue yet plausible, or do something to fool me. I stayed with a local family in the city centre, but arrived late at night, so the following morning I was still pretty sleepy and not thinking straight. I was informed that the youngest daughter had been keen to make my breakfast, and wanted to sit next to me and practise her English. So a very sweet little girl aged about six brought me my breakfast, which was delicious apart from a cup of very strong, and very cold, coffee. She looked so happy and pleased with herself that I decided not to say anything about the coffee, in case I upset her. The girl and her family watched me drink it all, and it wasn't until they all burst out laughing that I realised it was an April Fools' joke. I couldn't help but laugh then, too!

Sam in the USA

I was in New York for April Fools' Day. I knew to expect far-fetched stories in the media that would stretch most people's credibility. However, I still wasn't always quite sure whether what I was reading was true or not. There was a supposedly serious article about how a famous football player in his prime had decided to retire, which would actually have been quite plausible to a foreigner like myself had I not been very aware of the date. There was also a review of a new book by an actress that does not in fact exist, and a story about the introduction of a new milkshake-flavoured sauce, soon to be introduced by a fast-food chain. The latter was easier to discount than some, perhaps, but still felt almost possible. I wasn't fooled at all by the news about a new edible ice-cream face mask, but would that actually be so terrible?! And the advertisement for a perfume that smells like outer space was also fake, I discovered, as was the one for cauliflower-flavoured chocolate. That wasn't too much of a disappointment!

GRAMMAR
IMPERSONAL REPORTING STRUCTURES

1 Match the sentence halves.

1 There is said to be some misinformation about
2 Our student union president is said to have
3 It has been reported that the story
4 As many as 200 people were said
5 There were rumoured to be questions about the
6 The president's wife is believed to be shocked

a resigned his position at the meeting last night.
b credibility of the police's main witness.
c to have been taken in by the cybercriminal.
d comes from a very reliable source.
e our latest product being spread on social media.
f by the revelations about her husband's behaviour.

1 _____ 2 _____ 3 _____ 4 _____ 5 _____ 6 _____

2 Report the information using the words in bold in the correct form.

1 There's a **rumour** that schools will all be closed tomorrow.
It is _____.

2 The newspapers **say** that people have lost thousands of pounds in the scam.
Thousands _____.

3 The **belief** is that the economy will recover next year.
It is _____.

4 People **say** there is a lot of support for the new legislation.
There is _____.

5 We **thought** that Gabriel found the news shocking.
Gabriel _____.

6 Scientists **declared** the pandemic was over.
The pandemic _____.

STRUCTURES USED WITH REPORTING VERBS

3 Choose the correct options.

1 Morgan confessed to *writing* / *write* the hoax email.
2 My silence was misinterpreted *as* / *like* agreement.
3 He tends to exaggerate *on* / *about* how much money he makes.
4 I was reassured *that* / *how* my complaints would be listened to.
5 The politician is alleged *to making* / *to have made* fraudulent expense claims.
6 She denied *having* / *to have* eaten the last slice of cake.

4 Correct the mistakes in the sentences or put a tick by any you think are correct.

1 I confessed to the lecturer that I don't attend the previous day's class. _____
2 Greg is reputed to being an undercover police officer. _____
3 Why are you always going on about your film collection? _____
4 My cat was alleged to kill my neighbour's rabbit. _____
5 The ticket company reassured that we would get a refund. _____

PREPARE FOR THE EXAM

Reading and Use of English Part 1

5 Read the text below and decide which answer (A, B, C or D) best fits each gap. There is an example at the beginning (0).

Public Speaking

It has been **(0)** _claimed_ that there are two types of public speaker – those who admit to being nervous, and those who **(1)** _____ it. The fact of the matter is that everyone feels a **(2)** _____ amount of anxiety before speaking in front of an audience, even those who actually enjoy being the **(3)** _____ of attention at other times. The secret is to channel that nervous energy into making your performance the best it can possibly be.

Nevertheless, it can be useful to **(4)** _____ yourself that the audience is not actually interested in *you* personally. They are there to hear what you have to say, that is all. So you can relax. But do not get too relaxed, or your laid-back attitude could be **(5)** _____ as a lack of interest. You need to strike a **(6)** _____.

Another pitfall to avoid is **(7)** _____ on for too long. Remember the **(8)** _____ rule: always make sure you have finished speaking before your audience has finished listening!

0 A told	**B** demanded	**C** claimed	**D** kept
1 A deny	**B** reject	**C** refuse	**D** dismiss
2 A clear	**B** definite	**C** sure	**D** certain
3 A middle	**B** core	**C** heart	**D** centre
4 A confess	**B** reassure	**C** assert	**D** boast
5 A compared	**B** translated	**C** explained	
D misinterpreted			
6 A balance	**B** scale	**C** match	**D** level
7 A getting	**B** going	**C** passing	**D** moving
8 A silver	**B** perfect	**C** diamond	**D** golden

EXAM TIP

The words in the options are similar in meaning, but often used in different contexts. For example, some words can only be used to talk about people, and others only for objects or places.

VOCABULARY
PHRASAL VERBS AND NOUNS

1 Choose the correct options.

1 If people are doing something illegal, the authorities will have to *crack down on / turn over* it.
2 You can *pay out / go ahead* with something if you have been given permission to proceed.
3 A company or institution which makes a mistake may have to *tip off / pay out* large sums of money to people.
4 If you want to save money, you'll need to *cut back / tip off* the amount of money you spend on non-essential items.
5 If you give someone secret information, you are *tipping them off / turning them over*.
6 Profitable companies consistently *go ahead / turn over* a lot of money.

2 Complete the sentences with the phrasal verbs from Exercise 1 in the correct form.

1 My insurance company refused to _____ because the accident was my fault.
2 The local bookshop _____ a lot more than usual last year.
3 You'll need to _____ the number of calories you consume if you want to lose weight.
4 Do you think the new housing development will _____ , or will it be cancelled?
5 The police were _____ about a fraudster operating in the area.
6 Social media companies are being urged to _____ fake news being uploaded to their platforms.

3 Rewrite the sentences in Exercise 2 using the noun versions of the phrasal verbs.

1 Because the accident was my fault, I didn't receive *a payout from my insurance company* .
2 The local bookshop's _____ .
3 You're going to have to make _____ .
4 Do you think the new housing development will get _____ ?
5 The police received _____ .
6 Social media companies are being urged to implement _____ .

4 Match the sentence halves.

1 If your **outgoings** exceed your income,
2 The **turnover** of many businesses will suffer
3 To be given the **go-ahead** on our latest project
4 The **upkeep** of this large, historic building
5 We didn't make much money at the **outset**,
6 Being refused a loan from our bank

a would be the most desirable **outcome**.
b was a real **setback**.
c is extremely high.
d but our company became profitable within a year.
e if there's a **downturn** in the national economy.
f you will have financial difficulties.

1 _____ 2 _____ 3 _____ 4 _____ 5 _____ 6 _____

5 Complete the conversations with phrasal verbs and nouns from this page.

1 A: The _____ of this office building is costing my new company millions of euros.
   B: I could have told you that at the _____ . You're going to have to reduce your _____ somehow.
   A: I'm not sure if we can afford to make any more _____ !

2 A: The profits of social media companies have taken a _____ this year.
   B: And it will get worse if the government _____ with its plans to ban fake news being published online.
   A: Well, if a less toxic internet is the _____ , I'm not going to complain.

3 A: Bad news – the education board isn't going to _____ any more money to support adult literacy courses.
   B: Well, that's a bit of a _____ for us. But we can still run them without their help.

4 A: I've just had a _____ that the police are going to _____ on illegal parking in the area.
   B: I'm not surprised. The local council's annual _____ is falling, so they need to generate money from fines.

LISTENING

1 Do you think you can catch a cold by going out in cold weather? Why? / Why not?

_____

_____

2 You are going to listen to an interview about people believing things which are not true. Why do people adopt false beliefs? Can you think of any common ones?

_____

_____

3 Read question 1 below and underline the key words. Think about what the answer could be.

1 Donna says people believe untrue things because they

_____

4 Now look at the complete question 1 in Exercise 8. Do any of the options match your prediction?

 5 Listen to the first part of the interview and answer question 1 in Exercise 8.

6 Underline the part of the text which indicates the correct answer. Highlight any distractors.

> With the rise of the internet, there has been a huge growth in the adoption of false beliefs. We rely on it for so much these days, and the sheer volume of information available can be overwhelming. As to why false ideas are believed – whether they're bad science, conspiracy theories or simple internet hoaxes – it's not that people are stupid. Far from it. Highly intelligent people are as susceptible as anyone. The fact is that humans need explanations. This urge is behind every scientific advance in history. But it's easily misdirected.

7 Look at questions 2–6 in Exercise 8. Match them to their focus.

opinion _____

agreement _____

Listening Part 3

 8 You will hear an interview in which two experts called Donna Hubbard and Derek Barker are talking about why people believe things which are not true. For questions 1–6, choose the answer (A, B, C or D) which fits best according to what you hear.

1 Donna says people believe untrue things because they
  A depend too heavily on the internet.
  B are not able to deal with so much data.
  C feel they must understand why things happen.
  D lack the scientific skills required to know better.

2 When Derek talks about the relationship between the full moon and crime, he reveals his
  A annoyance at the police for spreading falsehoods.
  B amusement at the foolishness of the public.
  C regret that the story became popular.
  D frustration at the misuse of statistics.

3 On the link between the cold virus and cold weather, they both feel that
  A the idea is initially plausible.
  B it precedes the arrival of computers.
  C there is a scientific explanation for it.
  D the confusion is caused by the homophone.

4 Donna thinks it is difficult to remove a false belief because
  A it can cause emotional distress.
  B nobody likes admitting they were mistaken.
  C it involves a large amount of mental energy.
  D there is a natural hostility towards the unfamiliar.

5 According to Derek, what is the best way to avoid false beliefs?
  A Seek a diverse range of opinions.
  B Learn more about human psychology.
  C Question your own thought processes.
  D Be more selective in your information sources.

6 When talking about the future, they both believe that
  A the ways of spreading false information are multiplying.
  B people are more willing to believe anything.
  C the amount of misinformation is increasing.
  D education is vital for continued progress.

EXAM TIP

As preparation, it is useful to study reporting verbs, adjectives describing feelings and words used to report opinions and degrees of certainty.

READING AND USE OF ENGLISH

1 Match the phrasal verbs to the definitions.

1 take on   **2** take after   **3** take in   **4** take off

a trick or deceive
b start doing an activity or job
c be similar to an older member of your family
d remove an item of clothing

1 ....   **2** ....   **3** ....   **4** ....

2 Now look at the example (0) in Exercise 4. Are any of the following possible as an alternative answer? Why? / Why not?

A off   **B** after   **C** on

3 Which of the following is correct for gap 1? Why?

A faster   **B** easier   **C** harder   **D** clearer

PREPARE FOR THE EXAM

Reading and Use of English Part 2

4 Read the text below and think of the word which best fits each gap. Use only one word in each gap. There is an example at the beginning (0).

HOW TO SPOT A LIAR

Nobody likes being lied to. The feeling that you have been taken **(0)** _in_ by a liar is a deeply unpleasant one. Unfortunately, actually detecting when a person is lying to you is **(1)** .... said than done.

An internet search will return lots of tips about how to identify a liar. Most of these will relate **(2)** .... body language. For example, if a person looks up to the right while speaking, it is supposedly a sign that they are being untruthful. However, it could just as plausibly be put **(3)** .... to other things. Your innocent companion **(4)** .... well be telling the truth – they are just trying to remember something.

What *will* help to discern if someone is lying is if you know how the person **(5)** .... question normally acts. Perhaps a friend is behaving in **(6)** .... an unusual way that you suspect dishonesty. That does not constitute definite proof, but if **(7)** .... else, it could justify you asking, 'Is that true?'

That simple question is sometimes the most effective lie detector **(8)** .... all.

EXAM TIP

If you are not sure of the correct answer, have a guess.

5 Which of the following options means *to think that a situation is caused by a particular thing*?

1 put up with
2 put down to
3 put out of

6 Now complete question 1 in Exercise 8, using the correct phrasal verb from Exercise 5.

7 Each question in Part 4 of the *Reading and Use of English* section is worth 2 marks. This means you have to make two changes to the original sentence in your answer. Look again at question 1. What are the two changes you have to make?

....

PREPARE FOR THE EXAM

Reading and Use of English Part 4

8 For questions 1–6, complete the second sentence so that it has a similar meaning to the first sentence using the word given. Do not change the word given. You must use between three and six words, including the word given.

1 I think he is successful because he has wealthy parents.
DOWN
I put his .... wealthy parents.

2 Agreeing to the deal is the only thing you can do.
OPTION
You have .... agree to the deal.

3 There wasn't anything at all in the plans that he objected to.
ISSUE
He said there was absolutely .... with in the plans.

4 The attempted email scam did not fool anybody.
IN
Nobody .... the attempted email scam.

5 It was wrong of the police to arrest that young campaigner.
NOT
That young campaigner .... by the police.

6 Despite our hard work, we couldn't increase our turnover.
HOW
No ...., we couldn't increase our turnover.

EXAM TIP

Read your completed second sentence to check that your answer means the same as the first sentence.

9 Draw a line in your answers to Exercise 8 to separate the two changes that you made.

VOCABULARY AND READING
WORK AND CAREERS

1 Complete the sentences with the words in the box.

> appoint   climb   enterprise   hold   out   recruit
> resign   steady   vocation   well

1 This new _____ will boost the local economy.
2 You're very _____-qualified now, so I'm sure you'll find a good job soon.
3 They've finished interviewing people for the coaching job, so I'm sure they'll _____ someone soon.
4 It took my brother a long time to find a _____ job, but he's been working in sales for five years now.
5 Many people regard teaching as a _____ rather than simply a career.
6 They're planning to _____ a lot of people to help with the international football tournament here next year.
7 He's got such a bad attitude towards work – do you really think he'll be able to _____ **down a job**?
8 You should never _____ **from** your job before you've found another one.
9 Not everyone hopes to _____ **the corporate ladder** – some people enjoy having a relatively stress-free job.
10 If you're ever _____ **of a job**, contact me and I'll try to help.

2 Complete the sentences with a word or completed expression in bold from Exercise 1.

1 You need to settle down now and get _____.
2 She wants to _____ and become a top executive.
3 You have to be reliable if you want to _____ in this factory.
4 If you do this course, you'll be _____ for any job in the IT sector.
5 The business I worked for closed down, so now I'm _____.
6 If you want to work for this _____, you need to be highly motivated.
7 I do this job because I love it – I feel it's my _____.
8 I think my cousin's going to _____ her job – she doesn't enjoy it.
9 We're excited to find out who they've decided to _____ as head of department.
10 The business is doing well – we'll need to _____ some new staff soon.

3 Complete the sentences so that they are true for you.

1 I think I'm well-qualified to work as a _____.
2 I know someone whose vocation is _____.
3 If someone's out of a job, I think they should _____.
4 I think that being a _____ is a really good steady job.
5 To climb the corporate ladder, people often have to _____.

4 Read the first paragraph of the article on the opposite page. Why did Sarah Farnes start making ice cream?

A She no longer wanted to be a farmer.
B She needed to make some extra money.
C She met someone who knew how to make it.

5 Read the rest of the article, ignoring the gaps. Are the sentences T (True), F (False) or NM (Not Mentioned)?

1 Farnes found it difficult to make good ice cream at first. _____
2 Mace now makes the ice cream on her own. _____
3 Some flavours of ice cream are quicker to make than others. _____
4 Mace is equally busy making ice cream throughout the year. _____
5 Mace cleans the whole machine every time she finishes making a flavour. _____
6 Mace sometimes eats ice cream in her free time. _____

✓ PREPARE FOR THE EXAM

Reading and Use of English Part 7

6 Read the article again and choose from the paragraphs A–G the one which fits each gap (1–6). There is one extra paragraph which you do not need to use.

✓ EXAM TIP

After filling in the gaps, read the text through with the options to make sure that it makes complete sense.

7 Match the highlighted words or phrases in the text to the definitions.

1 without problems _____
2 stirred or beaten _____
3 a group of things that are made or dealt with at the same time _____
4 good at one's job _____
5 job opportunities _____

Chief Ice-Cream Maker

Reporter Mark King goes to a farm and meets an ice-cream maker.

If climbing the corporate ladder isn't for you, and you love food, perhaps a steady job as an ice-cream maker is something you might consider. For the past four years, Katy Mace has been chief ice-cream maker at a dairy farm close to her home. Sarah Farnes, who owns the farm, tells me that farming is an industry in which it can sometimes be hard to make ends meet, and five years ago, she was forced to think of other ways of keeping the farm profitable. Making and selling fresh ice cream was the resulting enterprise.

 1

Her arrival was lucky for all concerned. She and Farnes were already acquaintances, as their children attended the same school. Mace, who used to work in the banking sector, had mentioned she was interested in any local vacancies. As the ice cream became more and more popular, making so much of it grew too much for Farnes and her family to cope with. They looked for someone to recruit, and Mace was appointed chief ice-cream maker.

 2

Mixing everything together by hand is another of them, which is why Mace has an assistant to help, ensuring a smooth production line. Sugar and eggs are added to the milk and cream before the batch is given its particular flavour – strawberry, chocolate or, say, honeycomb. 'Chocolate is the hardest, as it's very thick and difficult to stir in.'

3

Once mixed, all the ingredients are added to the ice-cream machine. It heats the mixture to 84 °C for pasteurisation, and then cools it to as low as –12 °C , all in about 20 minutes. 'Flavours with more cream only need to be cooled to –9 °C because if they stayed in the machine any longer, they'd be churned into butter,' Mace explains.

4

Each batch Mace puts through the machine makes 10 litres of ice cream, and on a typical summer day she will produce 20–25 batches. In winter, though, when demand falls, she might only produce 200 litres a week.

5

On ice-cream-making days, Mace follows a strict colour order, putting through the lighter, creamier flavours (vanilla, honeycomb) first before moving on to the darker ice creams such as coffee, toffee and chocolate. 'If we didn't do that, we'd be rinsing every single part of the machine constantly,' Mace says.

 6

Mace admits that she often looks forward to making the darker varieties because that means the day is almost over. But she insists that her work can also be stimulating, and it does seem to have become a vocation. She has recently helped local school children develop innovative flavours for a competition, with the winning ice cream going on sale in a local supermarket. I wonder how much ice cream Mace herself eats. 'I don't eat a lot of it,' she says with a smile, 'because I'm here making it every day, but my youngest child loves it. If we go on holiday, I always have to taste the ice cream wherever we are, to see how it compares.'

A And also the messiest, Mace explains. 'If you get the slightest bit on you, before you know it, you find it's smeared everywhere – on your face, arms and legs.' She's sometimes picked the kids up from school covered in it. 'You do get some funny looks.'

B 'We've had some strange ones,' she laughs. She's made parmesan ice cream, lavender flavour and even a soy-sauce ice cream for a Chinese restaurant. 'Most taste surprisingly nice,' she says. She won't be out of a job any time soon, as she is clearly very competent.

C So she gets to help with other things then. 'I do some office work, and also drive the delivery van. It makes the work much more varied, which is nice.'

D It was a clever business decision, especially as the milk and cream that go into the product come from her herd of 160 cows, helping to keep costs down. The ice-cream division took off, and Mace soon came on board.

E Some of them also require additional ingredients, such as pieces of honeycomb. Mace says those are the ice creams that are harder to make. Anything with added bits takes extra time, whether it's white chocolate chips or pieces of fruit.

F I get the sense from this comment that the daily routine of preparing the ice cream can get quite boring: mixing the ingredients, filling the tubs, not to mention repeatedly cleaning and sterilising the equipment.

G 'It's certainly less stressful than my previous job,' she says, 'though it has its moments. In summer, we can't really produce enough ice cream, as the demand is crazy, or we might run out of lids or not have enough of one ingredient. So it has its own challenges.'

GRAMMAR
REPORTED QUESTIONS, OFFERS, REQUESTS AND SUGGESTIONS

1 Choose the correct options.

1 I asked her if *she was going / was she going* to resign.
2 She *wondered / asked* me why I wanted to know.
3 His boss wanted to know which candidate he *had appointed / appointed*.
4 He enquired how long I *had been / was* out of a job.
5 She asked him *whether / how* the candidate was well-qualified enough.
6 They wondered *why / how* I wasn't looking for a steady job.

2 Rewrite the sentences in Exercise 1 in direct speech.

1 _____
2 _____
3 _____
4 _____
5 _____
6 _____

3 Complete the sentences with verbs in brackets in the correct form.

1 My dad suggested _____ (phone) the leisure centre to see if they had any vacancies.
2 I offered _____ (help) him, but he said he was doing fine on his own.
3 He begged his boss _____ (let) him take an early holiday.
4 The careers advisor suggested that we _____ (apply) early for a summer job.
5 The manager suggested we _____ (work) weekends if we wanted to get promoted.
6 She suggested _____ (have) my CV designed by a professional.
7 We requested that someone _____ (bring) breakfast up to our room the next day.
8 The travel-agency manager offered _____ (reduce) the price of our holiday by 30%.

4 Complete the reported statements with the verbs *offer*, *ask* and *suggest* in the correct form.

1 'Will you post my application, please?'
She _____.
2 'Why don't you recruit some new salespeople?'
He _____.
3 'Please can you phone me when you get home?'
She _____.
4 'Would you like me to help you with your interview technique?'
He _____.
5 'Have you thought about finding a better paid job?'
She _____.
6 'Why don't we stay on holiday for another week?'
He _____.

5 Which of your answers from Exercise 4 are reported requests?

_____

 6 Correct the mistakes in the sentences or put a tick by any you think are correct.

1 We asked to the candidate why she wanted the job. _____
2 They suggested that I sending my application before the end of the week. _____
3 She wanted to know whether I intended to climb the corporate ladder. _____
4 I was advised to applying for a wide range of jobs. _____
5 The manager enquired why hadn't she phoned to say she'd be late. _____
6 I begged him appoint somebody to help me deal with all the work. _____

 PREPARE FOR THE EXAM

Reading and Use of English Part 4

7 Complete the second sentence so that it has a similar meaning to the first sentence, using the word given. Do not change the word given. You must use between three and six words, including the word given.

1 'Peter, you should ask the teacher to check your application for errors,' I said. **ADVISED**
I _____ checked for errors by the teacher.
2 I'd be interested to know why I didn't get a pay rise. **WONDER**
I _____ given a pay rise.
3 'Why is keeping a job an impossibility for you?' my father asked me. **DOWN**
My father asked me why I found _____ a job.
4 'Please don't ask me to work over the weekend, Sarah.' **BEGGED**
He _____ to work over the weekend.
5 'Are you going to follow your vocation?' she asked me. **KNOW**
She _____ going to follow my vocation.
6 They said that they would give me training before I started work. **PROMISED**
I _____ trained before I started work.

✓ EXAM TIP

This part of the exam tests your ability to express a message in a different way.

VOCABULARY
EXPRESSIONS WITH *WORK*

1 Match the two parts of the phrases.

1 work your	up
2 the	work of
3 have your work	way up
4 be worked	the clock
5 get down	to work
6 make short	works
7 do the	donkey work
8 working against	cut out

2 Match the definitions A–H to the phrases 1–8 from Exercise 1.

A finish something quickly _____

B be emotionally affected _____

C doing something in a limited amount of time _____

D start working _____

E have something difficult to do _____

F everything, including all the extras _____

G gradually move to a higher position _____

H do a boring, hard or repetitive job _____

3 Complete the conversations with *work* phrases from Exercise 1.

1 A: This thing has to be finished by tomorrow morning, so we'd better _____ .

B: Why do we always have to work _____ ? I'm so fed up with it.

A: Don't get _____ about it! It pays the bills.

2 A: We went out for a huge meal last night: starter, main course, dessert, cheese – _____ .

B: Did you eat it all?

A: Yes, I was absolutely starving, so I _____ of it!

3 A: I've just got a new job. It's not very well paid, but I intend to work _____ to the top.

B: You will have your _____ for you – there's a lot of people in that company trying to do the same.

A: I'll succeed because I'm determined not to spend the rest of my life doing _____ for other people.

COMPLEX PREPOSITIONS

4 Complete the sentences with the words in the box.

> accordance   ahead   behalf   charge   lack
> means   place   way

1 If you are in _____ with something, you follow its rules, laws or wishes.

2 To do something on _____ of somebody or something is to do it as their representative.

3 'In _____ of' is a more formal way of saying 'instead of'.

4 If you are in _____ of something, you are responsible for it.

5 If something happens or is done for _____ of something, it is because that thing was not available.

6 Another way to say 'as a type of' is 'by _____ of'.

7 '_____ of' means 'before'.

8 When you do A 'by _____ of' B, you use B to achieve A.

5 Complete the sentences with phrases from Exercise 4.

1 I need to speak to whoever is _____ this garage because I have a serious complaint.

2 If we work quickly, we should finish this project _____ the deadline.

3 _____ any better ideas, we decided to stay at home and watch TV that evening.

4 Are you sure this bridge was built _____ health and safety regulations? It doesn't look safe to me.

5 For this recipe, you can use oil _____ butter.

6 _____ the whole class, I would like to thank our teacher, Mrs Cummings, for her support.

7 More meetings are held _____ video conferencing these days.

8 I bought her a big bouquet of flowers _____ an apology.

6 Complete the sentences so that they are true for you.

1 I sometimes get worked up about _____ .

2 The last time I was in charge of something _____ .

3 Once, I spoke on behalf of _____ .

4 Working against the clock is something I _____ .

WRITING
A REPORT

» SEE *PREPARE TO WRITE* BOX, STUDENT'S BOOK PAGE 109

1 Do you know what job you want to do in the future? Put the following in order of importance.

   a doing interesting work ....
   b doing work that is considered important ....
   c being your own boss ....
   d having sociable hours ....
   e earning a high salary ....
   f working with the public ....
   g having long holidays ....
   h working in a team ....

2 What kinds of things are helpful for young people when they are choosing a career?

....

....

....

....

3 Read the task. How many sections should there be in your report?

> You recently attended a careers day at your college. Final-year students listened to talks by people with careers in a variety of fields and met careers advisers. Your headteacher has asked you to write a report about the event.
>
> In your report, you should explain what happened on the day, evaluate how helpful the event was for students and make recommendations for similar careers events at your college in the future.
>
> Write your **report**.

....

....

4 Read the sample answer. Write your own headings in gaps A–D. What do the verbs in bold have in common? Are they the most appropriate words to use in a report?

REPORT ON CAREERS DAY

A ....

Last week, our college held a day-long careers event. In the morning (9–12 am), final-year students could [1] **go to** sessions with careers advisers. In the afternoon (1–5 pm), there were talks by professionals – from restaurant managers to doctors. 80 students took part.

B ....

The event [2] **turned out** to be both enjoyable and useful. Students reported that the careers advice given in the morning was practical and constructive, and that the advisers were well-informed and supportive. Leaflets were also available on a selection of work options, and students were encouraged to help themselves to these. The talks in the afternoon were entertaining and instructive; the speakers took the perspective of students our age into account, and were happy to answer our questions.

C ....

There were only three careers advisers at the event. This meant that there was less than ten minutes available for each student, which was not enough time for an in-depth interview. As a result, the students spent the rest of the time reading the leaflets and chatting. The eight talks [3] **took** an hour each, and the two most popular speakers both [4] **gave** their talks from 2–3 pm.

D ....

It might be worth [5] **thinking about** inviting a greater number of careers advisers next year, [6] **giving** them more time with each student. It would also be useful to [7] **have** a list of speakers in advance for the students, then arrange the timetable with student input so that more people would have the chance to hear the talks of greatest interest to them. I would also recommend [8] **having** the talks in the morning, followed by the careers interviews. If that were [9] **done**, the former might usefully inform the latter; the students might learn things during the talks which could focus their minds during the careers interviews.

5 Replace the verbs in bold in the report using the verbs in the box in the correct form. Use each verb once only.

> allow   attend   consider   deliver   implement
> last   prove   provide   schedule

1	4	7 ....
2	5	8 ....
3	6	9 ....

6 Underline the structures used in the sample answer to give suggestions and recommendations. What verb forms follow them?

....

....

7 Choose the correct options.

1 My recommendations would include *inviting / invite / to invite* more speakers.

2 Another suggestion might be *you should cover / cover / to cover* a wider range of careers.

3 I suggest we *asking / ask / to ask* local artists to attend.

4 One student recommended *finding out / find out / to find out* what other colleges have done.

5 I think we *should change / change / changing* the timetable slightly.

6 It was suggested that all students *being given / were given / be given* name badges.

8 Read the question and plan your report. What job are you going to write about? Imagine spending a day with someone who does that job. Where would you go and what would you see? What would be useful about spending a day in this way?

> Your college recently arranged for you to spend a day with a professional of your choice at their workplace. Your headteacher has asked you to write a report about your experience.
> In your report, you should explain who you spent the day with, where you went and what you did. You should evaluate the experience and make recommendations that might help another student doing something similar in the future.
> Write your **report**.

....

....

....

....

PREPARE FOR THE EXAM

Writing Part 2

9 Write your report. Use some of the expressions you have learned to make suggestions and recommendations. Write 220–260 words.

EXAM TIP

You may want to present both positive and negative points in the same paragraph. Use the plan that makes the most sense for the report you are going to write.

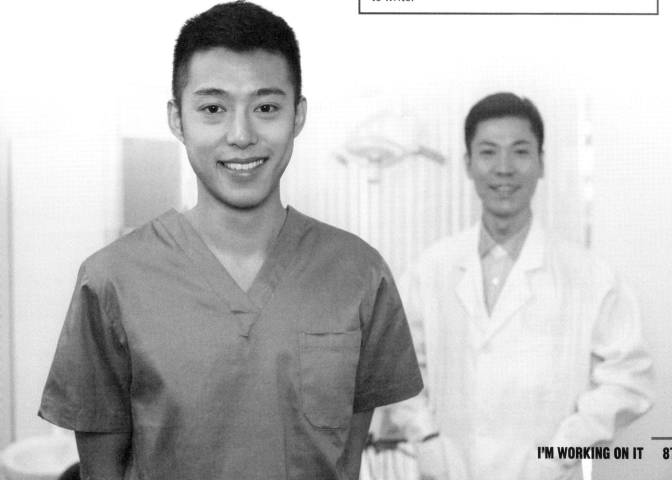

15 BORN TO LEAD

VOCABULARY AND READING
HEROES AND LEADERS

1 **Complete the sentences. The first letter of each missing word is given.**

1 I think that c_____ for human rights will eventually succeed in improving society.

2 Jo decided to organise a march because somebody needed to **take the i**_____.

3 It's sometimes better to be a little flexible rather than totally u_____.

4 You can be an a_____ for a good cause by talking to people about it and trying to convince them of its benefits.

5 I admire her confidence – she's so s_____ – a_____.

6 The organisation needs to find a good s_____ to explain their ideas to the press.

7 Not many people have heard of him, but he's one of the great u_____ h_____ of the peace movement.

8 She always knows what to do in difficult situations – she's very r_____.

9 Do people suffering from the worst effects of climate change need a famous actor to **be a v**_____ **for** them?

10 My parents are highly c_____ to helping reduce plastic waste in our community.

2 **Complete the sentences with a word or completed expression in bold from Exercise 1.**

1 His success has helped him to _____ people who are less well-off than he is.

2 I used to be very shy, but recently I've become far more _____.

3 Many human-rights activists were _____, and completely forgotten by history.

4 My sister spends most of her free time working for a charity. She's extremely _____.

5 People of all ages are now becoming climate-change _____ and taking part in demonstrations.

6 The new _____ for our animal-rights group has just been interviewed on TV.

7 Nothing will make him change his mind about using disposable plastic – he's totally _____ regarding that subject.

8 I'm sure she'll come up with a solution – she's very _____.

3 **Read the article on the opposite page, quickly. Which of the following could be an alternative title?**

A Izzy Christiansen supports a good cause

B A change of career for Izzy Christiansen

C Izzy Christiansen plans to set up a foundation

4 **Read the first paragraph of the article again. For question 1 in Exercise 5, decide which answer (A, B, C or D) best fits each gap. Underline the part(s) of the text which helped you to find the answer.**

PREPARE FOR THE EXAM

Reading and Use of English Part 5

5 **Read the rest of the article and decide which answer (A, B, C or D) best fits each gap.**

1 What does the writer say about Christiansen in the first paragraph?

A She has sometimes felt herself to be an unsung hero.

B Recent events have forced her to become more resourceful.

C She is accustomed to situations in which she needs to take the initiative.

D She is uncompromising when it comes to keeping up with her training.

2 What is suggested in the second paragraph?

A Women are generally more committed as activists than men often are.

B Common Goal campaigners target women more often than men for donations.

C Common Goal should work harder to attract support from both men and women.

D Women in football are more eager to help others than their male colleagues are.

3 What does the use of the phrase 'this is not virtue signalling' in line 31 highlight?

A that having first-hand experience of a problem is of value

B that Christiansen's motives for supporting good causes are genuine

C that there's a need for more people to be strong advocates for human rights

D that medical professionals like Christiansen's sister have a positive attitude to charities

4 What is the writer doing in the fourth paragraph?

A demonstrating some of Christiansen's weaknesses

B explaining why Christiansen chose to change teams

C justifying Christiansen's doubts about her career as a footballer

D providing a further opportunity to understand Christiansen's character

5 What does Christiansen say in the fifth paragraph about joining Common Goal?

A She believes she had a responsibility to do it.

B She has sometimes felt less self-assured since doing it.

C She regrets that so few other players have done it.

D She was persuaded to do it by one of its spokespersons.

6 What feeling is conveyed in the final paragraph?

A a slight lack of willingness to face reality

B an intense desire to resume a previous lifestyle

C a dissatisfaction with entertainment options available

D a powerful urge to improve future prospects

EXAM TIP

The options will not usually contain the same words as the text – don't try to match words in the options to those in the text to find the answer.

Izzy Christiansen, British football player

Izzy Christiansen knows so much about living with relentless pressure that making significant, split-second decisions comes as second nature. It is all just another part of her job as an Everton and England footballer. For the moment, though, there are no adrenaline highs, no trophies to pursue and no need to provide constant proof she deserves her place in the starting lineup. On one level, time out because of injury has been immensely frustrating, but it has also afforded the 28-year-old midfielder time to reflect on a renewed love for the game and a new-found determination to promote social justice.

Christiansen has joined Common Goal, a collective social-impact movement enabling anyone involved in the world game to donate at least 1% of their salary to a network of football-based community projects supporting young people in more than 90 countries. Of the 153 players and managers signed up, more than 50% are female. Considering the often vast difference in salaries for men and women, that represents quite a statement. As Christiansen sits at home, addressing a Zoom-linked computer screen against a backdrop of French art before preparing to head out for one-to-one training with a conditioning coach, she looks anything but surprised. 'It's really important to women footballers that we're role models,' she says. 'It gives you an insight into the type of people we are. We've fought battles throughout our careers to change perceptions. Common Goal is so relevant to us.'

The sincerity radiating through the screen emphasises that this is not virtue signalling, a point which is reinforced when it becomes apparent that her desire to support sanitation projects, to ensure the provision of clean water and toilet facilities all over the world, is intensely personal. Her younger sister, Rosie, who recently graduated from medical school in Glasgow, Scotland, is working long, stressful hours on hospital wards as part of her studies, prior to qualifying as a doctor. 'My sister did a Master's degree in tropical medicine,' Christiansen says. 'It sparked my interest in Common Goal projects and how they can help sanitation across the world.'

Christiansen's life as a sportsperson has not always been easy, and like many of her peers, she has had to learn to deal with disappointment. Before she joined the English team Everton, she played for the French team Lyon. She went through a difficult time there initially, and even briefly considered quitting the game. Then, after a successful season with them, she fractured her leg and damaged her ankle ligaments. As a result, she had to miss that summer's World Cup.

Norway's Ada Hegerberg, another Lyon player, helped Christiansen through the dark days, and influenced her decision to join Common Goal. 'I'm the first Everton player to join, so I'd like to think it can set an example to my teammates because football's a really powerful tool for change,' Christiansen says. 'Ada's someone I look up to; she's not afraid to speak up and fight for what she believes in. I've always had a voice – I just haven't necessarily had the confidence to use it. But now, I think that if you believe in something, or can contribute to change for the better, then it's important to speak up. As footballers, we're in a very privileged position. People look up to us. We have to make sure we deliver key messages.'

Christiansen cannot wait to get back to playing football. She says that as she recovers from her injury, the days have just drifted by; she has not felt she knew where they were going – she has not even watched much TV, but has done a lot of walking and reading. She is keen to be back, and optimistic about the future of women's football. 'Women's Super League players are world-class – teams are getting stronger,' she says. 'I'm constantly looking ahead now. I can't wait to get back to training, to a normal routine and weekend fixtures. When it's taken away, you realise how much you miss it.'

---

6 Match the highlighted words or phrases in the text to the definitions.

1 something which helps you to achieve your aims _____
2 try to obtain _____
3 passed without the feeling that anything significant was happening _____
4 started _____
5 coming across strongly / clearly visible _____

GRAMMAR
ELLIPSIS AND SUBSTITUTION

1 Cross out unnecessary words from the sentences.

1 I am committed to fighting for human rights, and my partner is committed to human rights, too.

2 She has contacted the local council and has complained about the pollution.

3 The speech he made last night was one of his most uncompromising speeches.

4 I left a note on the kitchen table and I drove to the airport.

5 The largest demonstration that I ever attended was in London.

6 They called off the protest, but it isn't clear why they called off the protest.

7 Simon is a very resourceful campaigner, and Greta is a very resourceful campaigner as well.

8 We are grateful for your support and are hopeful that change is coming soon.

2 What was crossed out in the sentences 1–8 in Exercise 1?

A nouns and noun phrases ....

B verbs (including auxiliary verbs) ....

C pronouns (including relative pronouns) ....

D clauses ....

3 Complete the sentences with the words in the box.

> any   do so   every one   neither   one   that
> the same   those

1 I have some leaflets about climate change. Would you like ....?

2 Both her parents are very well off, but unfortunately .... is interested in environmental issues.

3 Our campaign has succeeded in raising awareness among the general public, and .... is what really matters.

4 A few people might disagree with our methods, but I don't know .... who would object to our aims.

5 Our group would like to send a delegate to the conference, but we don't have the finances to ....

6 Not everyone likes extremely committed campaigners, but .... are the kind who change the world.

7 There were quite a few protests last year, and I went to ....

8 Greg wrote a letter to the local paper, and his partner did ....

4 Substitute the parts of the sentence in italics.

1 The authorities told everyone to remain in their homes, but nobody *remained in their homes*. ....

2 My grandfather was a voice for the oppressed, and I want to be *a voice for the oppressed* too. ....

3 A lot of people believe global warming is a myth. *The belief that global warming is a myth* is not true. ....

4 I have made two speeches in my life, and *the two speeches* were well received. ....

5 Alex needs to pass all of his exams, and I *also need to pass all of my exams.* ....

6 My mother has a car and a bicycle, but *the car and the bicycle aren't* battery powered. ....

5 Correct the mistakes in the sentences or put a tick by any you think are correct.

1 My partner has more time for activism than what I do. ....

2 Keeping up with the news is something I have always done so. ....

3 I've wanted an electric bike for ages, so I was delighted when I got it for my birthday. ....

4 Inspiring leaders can change the course of history, and few are as inspirational as Mandela. ....

5 The officers asked to see her travel documents, but she didn't have some. ....

6 His parents are committed environmentalists, but he isn't as interested in it as they. ....

PREPARE FOR THE EXAM

Reading and Use of English Part 2

6 Read the text below and think of the word which best fits each gap. Use only one word in each gap. There is an example at the beginning (0).

MY FIRST DEMO

I had never **(0)** *been* on a demonstration before. In fact, it wasn't **(1)** .... a politically active friend of mine told me that a climate-change march would take place in June that I even thought of going on one. I feel very strongly about climate change, and I think most people my age feel the **(2)** .... So I decided to join her and her group of campaigners.

I asked my parents if they wanted to go to the demo too, but **(3)** .... was interested. Fortunately, they had no objections to me **(4)** .... so. 'Just don't get into any trouble!' they said.

(5) .... piece of advice was well meant, but entirely unnecessary. Although there were tens of thousands of highly committed people there, absolutely **(6)** .... misbehaved in any way. There were a lot of children too, which is not surprising because they are the ones **(7)** .... future will be most affected by climate change. They have **(8)** .... to lose – and to gain – than their parents do.

EXAM TIP

Sometimes, from a grammatical point of view, it might look like it is not necessary to add a word – if you think that, be sure to look at the meaning of the whole sentence again to see if a negative (e.g. *no, not*) is required.

VOCABULARY
METAPHORS, SIMILES AND EUPHEMISMS

1 Choose the correct options.

1 My grandad looks a bit mean, but he actually has a heart of *gold / star*.
2 With a good manager, this office could *run / work* like clockwork.
3 As a company director, she took no *fools / prisoners* and was feared by many.
4 Thank you for all your hard work today – you have been an absolute *star / gold*.
5 One day, he's screaming at you to work harder, and the next day, he's as sweet as *gold / pie*.
6 We're going to have to work our *feet / socks* off if we want to finish this on time.
7 Our plan will succeed as long as nobody gets cold *feet / fish* at the last minute.
8 The year 2020 was a real *roller-coaster ride / fish out of water* for many people.
9 It took me a few minutes to *pull / push* myself together after the accident.
10 When he first started at the company, he felt like a *fish out of water / heart of gold*, but he soon settled in.

2 Complete the sentences with the euphemisms, similes and metaphors from Exercise 1.

1 If you _____, you suddenly become too afraid or nervous to do something.
2 When someone has a very pleasant manner, we say that they are _____.
3 A kind and generous person can be said to have a _____.
4 When you want to praise somebody for doing well, you can call them an absolute _____.
5 If something functions efficiently and on time, it _____.
6 An informal way of saying 'work very hard' is '_____'.
7 If someone is very direct in what they argue for, with little regard for others' feelings, we say they _____.
8 If someone feels out of place or uncomfortable in a particular environment, we say they are like a _____.
9 We say something is a _____ if it changes from one extreme to another, which may cause a person's feelings to change in the same way.
10 To _____ means to calm down after being angry or upset.

3 Match the euphemisms to the definitions.

1	on the streets	old
2	pass away	homeless
3	leave a lot to be desired	the toilet
4	getting on a bit	die
5	pre-owned	going bald
6	be economical with the truth	tell lies
7	not suffer fools gladly	very bad
8	the rest room	intolerant
9	going a bit thin on top	unemployed
10	between jobs	used

1 _____	6 _____
2 _____	7 _____
3 _____	8 _____
4 _____	9 _____
5 _____	10 _____

4 Complete the conversations with euphemisms from Exercise 3.

1 **A:** I used to have lots of hair, but now I'm beginning to _____.
   B: That's because you're _____. It happens to us all!

2 **A:** Did you hear the sad news? That homeless guy _____ last night.
   B: Poor man. He'd been _____ for years.

3 **A:** Stefan is a good boss, but his taste in clothes _____.
   B: I know! I don't understand why he doesn't buy new ones. Everything he wears looks _____.

4 **A:** I think our new company director is really going to shake things up. People say he doesn't _____ – so if you make a mistake, you'd better watch out!
   B: Hmm. I don't trust him. I've heard he can be manipulative, and even _____ if it means he can get what he wants.

5 Match the two halves of the similes.

1	as quick as _____	a feather
2	as solid as _____	a dog
3	as black as _____	lightning
4	as safe as _____	thunder
5	as regular as _____	new
6	as quiet as _____	a sheet
7	as good as _____	houses
8	as light as _____	a mouse
9	as white as _____	clockwork
10	as sick as _____	a rock

6 Rewrite the sentences using a simile from Exercise 5.

1 This weighs very little.
....
2 You look extremely pale.
....
3 Don't make any noise.
....
4 This butter is too hard.
....
5 He's very fast.
....
6 I feel extremely ill.
....

LISTENING

1 What are the people doing in the picture below? Would you join a campaign group? Why? / Why not?

....

....

....

....

2 Look at Task One in Exercise 6. What could the speakers say that has the same meaning as each item (A–H)?

....

....

....

....

....

....

3 Now listen to Speaker 1 and complete items 1 and 6 in Exercise 6.

4 Read what Speaker 1 says and underline the parts which give you the correct answers to items 1 and 6.

> We've always been a political family, although I was never particularly active. It's what I'm doing at uni – philosophy, politics and economics. For my final project, I chose to examine student political activism, and joined a student politics society to see how they operated. I wasn't an impostor – I shared the political views of the group, pretty much. They were a committed bunch, I'll give them that. Unfortunately, their commitment frequently expressed itself in furious arguments among themselves over what seemed to me to be trivial differences. As a result, the group was almost entirely ineffectual. It was a useful learning experience, but membership is *not* something I'll put on my CV!

5 Look again at what Speaker 1 says in Exercise 4. Highlight the parts which might mislead you to the wrong answer.

✓ PREPARE FOR THE EXAM

Listening Part 4

6 You'll hear five short extracts in which people are talking about being part of a campaigning organisation.

TASK ONE

For questions 1–5, choose from the list (A–H) the main reason each speaker gives for joining the organisation.

A the desire to broaden their social circle	
B the encouragement of a relative	
C the influence of a public figure	**1** Speaker 1 ....
D anger at an injustice	**2** Speaker 2 ....
E a need to feel useful	**3** Speaker 3 ....
F completion of a course of study	**4** Speaker 4 ....
G a means to improve career prospects	**5** Speaker 5 ....
H concern about the future	

TASK TWO

For questions 6–10, choose from the list (A–H) how each speaker felt about the campaigning organisation after they joined.

A put off by their extremism	
B pleased by the sense of solidarity	
C doubtful about their credibility	**6** Speaker 1 ....
D disappointed by their inability to	**7** Speaker 2 ....
effect change	**8** Speaker 3 ....
E frustrated by the lack of urgency	**9** Speaker 4 ....
F relieved to be among like-minded	**10** Speaker 5 ....
people	
G excited by the energetic attitude	
H optimistic about the prospect of success	

✓ EXAM TIP

When practising this part, try answering Task One and Task Two separately on each listening. Then try answering both tasks at the same time on each listening. Find out which method works best for you, and use it in the exam.

READING AND USE OF ENGLISH

1 Complete the sentences with the words in the box.

in (x2) into to

1 Our little meeting developed .... quite a party!
2 We hope this campaign will result .... a change of government policy.
3 The protest led .... several people being arrested.
4 I have a feeling this plan will end .... disaster.

2 Now look at gap 2 in Exercise 3 and the options below. Which option would you choose? Why?

....

✗ PREPARE FOR THE EXAM

Reading and Use of English Part 1

3 Read the text below and decide which answer (A, B, C or D) best fits each gap. There is an example at the beginning (0).

HIDE THE **PAIN** HAROLD

On the internet, everyone is trying to be famous. But what if you achieve fame by **(0)** *accident* ? That is what happened to András Aráto when he found himself in the **(1)** .... after some professionally taken photos of him **(2)** .... to his face becoming a meme.

The sixty-something Hungarian had made a little money by **(3)** .... for a commercial photographer. Although he was smiling in the photos, András **(4)** .... over as a deeply sad man who was trying to put on a brave face. Someone anonymously reposted the photos on social media with the words, 'Harold struggles not to let the pain **(5)** .... But the smile can only hide so much.'

'Hide the Pain Harold' became a viral **(6)** ....

At first, András wanted it all to stop – but he discovered that complaints about such things have no **(7)** .... Eventually, he came to **(8)** .... with it, and after a few years, started living the life of an international celebrity!

0 A fortune	**B** accident	**C** fate	**D** incident
1 A moonlight	**B** daylight	**C** flashlight	**D** spotlight
2 A led	**B** resulted	**C** developed	**D** ended
3 A staying	**B** presenting	**C** posing	**D** positioning
4 A came	**B** went	**C** stayed	**D** looked
5 A see	**B** show	**C** view	**D** demonstrate
6 A attraction	**B** eruption	**C** commotion	**D** sensation
7 A affect	**B** change	**C** effect	**D** result
8 A agreement	**B** terms	**C** acceptance	**D** peace

> ## ✓ EXAM TIP
>
> If you can, think of a word that might fit each gap without looking at the options.

4 Complete the table.

noun	adjective	verb	opposite adjective
....	exemplary	exemplify	—
resourcefulness	....	—	unresourceful
suitability	....	suit	....

5 Look at gaps 1–3 in Exercise 6. What part of speech is required in each? Which requires an opposite?

1 ....   3 ....
2 ....

✓ PREPARE FOR THE EXAM

Reading and Use of English Part 3

6 For questions 1–8, read the text below. Use the word given in capitals at the end of some of the lines to form a word that fits in the gap in the same line. There is an example at the beginning (0).

⭐🙌⭐ Role Models 🔍

What makes a good role model? You might think it depends on your own **(0)** *aspirations* . If you want to be a teacher, your role model will be a teacher who **(1)** .... all the qualities of the profession: patience, knowledge, **(2)** ...., etc. However, a recent survey shows that a large number of young people choose professional athletes as their role models, which would appear to be **(3)** .... for anyone who does not have an ambition to achieve sporting **(4)** ....

But sports professionals can be **(5)** .... role models. The discipline and control they **(6)** .... display on the field of play is certainly something worth emulating, whichever life path you choose. What is more, some of them have a strong sense of social responsibility, campaigning tirelessly and **(7)** .... to improve the lives of those less well off than themselves.

This contrasts with another popular source of role models – reality TV. Most 'famous-for-being-famous' celebrities lack the **(8)** .... of someone who has achieved fame through talent and hard work.

ASPIRE
EXAMPLE
RESOURCE

SUIT
STAR

STAND
CONTINUE

COMPROMISE

CREDIBLE

> ## ✓ EXAM TIP
>
> If the gapped word is an adjective or an adverb, think carefully about whether a positive or negative meaning is needed.

VOCABULARY AND READING
WORK AND STUDY

1 Match the definitions to the words and phrases in the box.

> apply yourself   assignment   dissertation
> humanities   intern   learn the ropes   numeracy
> on-the-job training   schooling   trade   workshop

1 find out how to do a job _____
2 someone who is training by getting practical experience of a job _____
3 subjects that are not a science, such as art, literature or history _____
4 work hard at something _____
5 a long piece of writing on a particular subject, especially one that is done in order to receive a university or college degree _____
6 a job, often one that requires special skills and involves working with your hands _____
7 learning about a job by doing it _____
8 knowing how to do maths _____
9 a piece of work that someone is told to do _____
10 an event in which people learn more about something by discussing it and doing practical exercises _____
11 primary and secondary education _____

2 Complete the sentences with a word or phrase from Exercise 1.

1 I'm going to a _____ tomorrow to learn more about dealing with customer complaints.
2 I think that _____ is the best way to improve your skills.
3 The teacher gives us an _____ to do every week.
4 My brother is an _____ with an IT company at the moment.
5 Every student has to do a _____ in their third year – it usually takes about two months to finish it.
6 Everyone needs basic _____ skills, such as adding and subtracting.
7 How long did it take you to _____ when you started working in the shoe factory?
8 I did most of my _____ abroad because my parents travelled a lot for work.
9 My school taught _____ better than the sciences, but I still became a doctor.
10 My father encouraged me to learn a _____ like furniture making, but I trained as an art teacher instead.
11 The only way to make progress in this field is to _____ and study a lot.

3 Read the article on the opposite page, quickly. Does each person mention where they are studying? If they do, where is it?

_____
_____

PREPARE FOR THE EXAM

Reading and Use of English Part 8

4 Read the article again and answer the questions.

Which person

1 offers a justification for being flexible about when people leave school? _____
2 thinks more time should be allowed for decisions about education? _____
3 advocates better communication between employers and educational establishments? _____
4 gives examples of the benefits of mixed-age classes? _____
5 dismisses arguments for restricting access to some subjects? _____
6 describes a refusal to accept an alternative point of view? _____
7 warns against underestimating those without formal qualifications? _____
8 criticises an unwillingness to consider changes to the school curriculum? _____
9 speculates on the reasons why some people are put off further education? _____
10 clarifies that some work experience only lasted for a short time? _____

 EXAM TIP

Sometimes, the information you need comes from a short phrase in the text, but more frequently, you will need to read several lines of text to get the answer.

5 Match the **highlighted** words or phrases in the text to the definitions.

1 unwise _____
2 signed up to attend classes _____
3 great skill, ability and experience _____
4 interested and involved in something _____
5 accept a responsibility or job _____

A LINDA

In my country, not everyone my age thinks that going to university is something they want to do. I suspect that one of the main issues is the fact that universities charge such high fees, and many school leavers are therefore reluctant to take on the large amount of debt that obtaining a degree will almost certainly involve, preferring to learn a trade instead. I think it is a pity that those who do decide to go often have to make crucial choices, such as what to study or where to study, over a period of just a few months. Their ambitions may also be limited by choices made three or four years earlier in their schooling, such as whether to focus on the sciences or humanities. This requirement to specialise so early takes no account of the huge changes that teenagers' brains undergo between making these choices and leaving school. It can also lead to cutting down on things like music and drama classes. There are those who say these should only be available to students who have musical or acting potential, but that has always seemed like nonsense to me because they encourage creativity and develop social skills.

I've been doing a school project about education systems in different countries around the world, and what strikes me is the huge variations between them – the age at which children start school, how they are taught, and so on. Generally, students seem to achieve well, within this wide range of settings. That's not to say that there's no room for improvement, however. Yet, when there have been calls at various times over the last few years in my country for a review of the subjects taught at primary and secondary level, there has been no response at all, which seems unreasonable. One approach I came across while researching for my project is having different generations learning together at school. In some parts of the world, grandparents who never had the chance to fully develop their literacy or numeracy skills have enrolled at school to learn alongside their grandchildren. This has apparently had a positive effect on the children's behaviour, and also boosted their confidence. I'd love to be involved in initiatives like that one day.

B YANIS

C HESTER

I've just started training as a teacher, and at a workshop the other day, we were discussing the end-of-year exams in secondary schools in my country. Someone suggested allowing students a free choice as to whether or not to take these. Some people just laughed and said that was ridiculous. They wouldn't even discuss it. Although I was a bit shocked too at first, I do think it's a concept worth exploring. Another idea that came up was allowing secondary-school students over the age of 14 to decide for themselves if they no longer wanted to continue in full-time education. I think that if students have more control over what happens in education, they are more likely to feel engaged, and as a result, apply themselves more willingly. I actually think that most pupils would choose to take exams, anyway, and stay on if they felt they were still learning valuable skills. And those who left but regretted it later could return and study again, alongside younger classmates.

As part of my university course, I'm currently doing an assignment on the benefits of on-the-job training for teenagers who have left school and decided not to go on to further education. I was an intern myself at a theatre company for a few months between school and university, but that was a slightly different matter, as I never intended to stay there long-term. However, it did allow me to learn the ropes, and gave me some useful insights into the world of work. Now I'm a student, I feel quite cut off from the *real world*. I feel it would make sense for industry and other sectors to interact more closely with schools, colleges and universities, to make sure that students leave with the skills needed to thrive in our ever-changing world. Proficiency in any area of work cannot be guaranteed by certificates or diplomas. In fact, many of the older people I worked with at the theatre company had none, and yet it would be extremely misguided to discount either their wisdom or expertise.

D THEO

GRAMMAR
REGRETS, WISHES AND PREFERENCES

1 Choose the correct options.

1 I wish I *chose / had chosen* a different topic for my dissertation.

2 To be honest, I'd rather you *didn't go / hadn't gone* in to work tomorrow.

3 Sally says she'd sooner not *attend / to attend* the workshop today.

4 If only I *accepted / had accepted* that intern position last week!

5 I wish Dave would *apply / have applied* himself to his studies more – he's got exams next week!

6 I'd rather *learn / learned* the ropes by working instead of doing a course.

7 I wish you didn't *have / had* to go back to Germany next month.

2 Match the sentence halves.

1 If only I hadn't
2 She would
3 I'd rather
4 I wish I didn't
5 He wishes he
6 I wish you

a have to finish this assignment.
b decided to give up formal education.
c had been given more on-the-job training.
d learn a trade and start earning some money.
e sooner get a job as a paid intern.
f didn't criticise my poetry.

1 .... 3 .... 5 ....
2 .... 4 .... 6 ....

3 Complete the sentences with the verbs in the box in the correct form.

> can   have   decide   pay   play   not play   read
> start   study

1 I wish my brother .... his music so loud in the mornings.

2 Steven wishes he .... to find a job instead of going to university.

3 If only I .... speak a foreign language!

4 Would you rather .... humanities or sciences?

5 Rachel says she'd sooner .... a good novel than .... a computer game.

6 He has always wished that he .... a more interesting job.

7 When you get a job, I hope you .... making a contribution towards paying the bills.

8 My numeracy is poor – I should .... more attention in maths class.

4 Complete the sentences. More than one answer is possible.

1 Somebody is playing the drums too loudly.
I wish they ....

2 I don't have many friends.
If only ....

3 I think football is better than basketball.
I'd sooner ....

4 I don't want to go to bed.
I'd rather ....

5 It's raining.
If only ....

6 I didn't get the job.
I wish ....

⊙ 5 Correct the mistakes in the sentences or put a tick by any you think are correct.

1 I hope of finding out who my roommate is soon.
....

2 If only I have a car – I could have picked you up from the station. ....

3 She'd much rather to go home early than stay till 5 pm. ....

4 I wish I'd been kinder to my little brother when we were young. ....

5 Darren wishes he hasn't promised to help with my dissertation. ....

6 Frankly, I'd sooner not spent so much on a pair of shoes. ....

6 Complete the sentences so that they are true for you.

1 If only I hadn't ....
2 I'd rather my teacher ....
3 I'd sooner .... than ....
4 I wish I had known ....
5 I wish I was ....
6 If only I had ....

VOCABULARY
COMPOUND ADJECTIVES

1 Unscramble the first part of the compound adjectives and match them with the second. Add a hyphen where necessary.

1 ounsd
2 ekil
3 abord
4 mitinav
5 hathel
6 nert
7 sestrs
8 tretes
9 strut
10 trawe

conscious
free (x2)
minded (x2)
proof (x2)
rich
wise
worthy

2 Complete the sentences with compound adjectives from Exercise 1.

1 Since I got a job, I can no longer live .... with my parents – they make me pay £50 a week.
2 I really need a .... week away from all of this pressure.
3 I only found out my new jacket wasn't .... when I got caught in the rain.
4 Sally is so .... that she goes to the gym every day and records everything she eats on an app.
5 I like to go on political demonstrations because it feels good to be with .... people.
6 Nobody wants to do business with my uncle because they don't think he is .... He's been accused of tricking people in the past.
7 Unless you are very ...., I don't recommend walking through that part of the city. You need to be constantly alert.
8 People who eat .... fruit and vegetables are healthier.
9 Colin won't listen to anyone whose opinion is different from his own because he isn't very ....
10 Fortunately, our hotel room was ...., so our sleep wasn't disturbed by the fireworks which went on throughout the night.

VERB SUFFIXES

3 Complete the table using the root word and the suffixes in the box.

(-ate   -en   -ide   -ify   -ise)

verb	adjective	noun
1	presidential	president
2	intense	intensification
3	frightening	fright
4	theoretical	theory
5	estimated	estimation

4 Complete the sentences with the correct verb form of the words in brackets.

1 Everyone who .... (resident) in the apartment block was informed that there was going to be a fire drill.
2 The council faced objections to the plans to .... (wide) the road outside the school.
3 We will have to .... (economy) if we are going to have enough money to go on holiday next year.
4 I have never been able to watch horror movies because they .... (terror) me so much.
5 My uncle likes to .... (demonstration) how quickly he can change a car tyre.
6 The time has come for you to .... (decisive) what you want to study.
7 Going to university will .... (broad) your horizons.
8 Rudeness is something that the teacher does not .... (tolerance).

✓ PREPARE FOR THE EXAM

Reading and Use of English Part 3

5 For questions 1–8, read the text below. Use the word given in capitals at the end of some of the lines to form a word that fits in the gap in the same line. There is an example at the beginning (0).

Working abroad ✈

For many young people, the idea of working abroad for a period is very **(0)** _attractive_ . You can brush up your language skills, experience a different culture, **(1)** .... with people from all over the world and maybe even save a bit of money if you want to. What is more, they say travel **(2)** .... the mind – so what have you got to lose?	ATTRACT SOCIAL BROAD
There are some obstacles you will need to **(3)** .... first. Apart from your job application, there may be a lot of other paperwork involved.	COME
The importance of getting all the right documents in order must not be **(4)** .... Visa, health insurance, driving licence, a bank account – the amount of form-filling required can be quite **(5)**	ESTIMATE COURAGE
For this reason, a **(6)** .... adventurer is well advised to sign up with an agent who can **(7)** .... the whole process for them. Most agents offer a wide **(8)** .... of overseas employment opportunities. But they will charge a fee, so do some research to find the most suitable one first.	PROSPECT SIMPLE DIVERSE

✓ EXAM TIP

Before taking the exam, practise making as many words as you can based on a common word (e.g. *know*, *question*).

WRITING
AN EMAIL OF APPLICATION

» SEE *PREPARE TO WRITE* BOX, STUDENT'S BOOK PAGE 123

1 Have you ever applied for a job? What do you think you have to do to apply for a job?

_____

_____

2 Do you think you would enjoy working in the film industry? What would be good and bad about such a career?

_____

_____

_____

_____

3 Read the task. What would make you suitable for this job?

> This leaflet is delivered to your home:
>
> > I am an English film producer making a film in your area this summer.
> > I am looking for a local person to work for two weeks to do the following:
> > • Act as a language interpreter for the director and me.
> > • Help to recruit people for crowd scenes.
> > • Help to identify good locations for filming.
> > Apply in writing to me, Anna Yellin (contact details overleaf).
>
> You decide to apply.
> Write your **application**.

_____

_____

_____

4 Read the sample answer, ignoring the gaps. Put the paragraphs A–D in the correct order.

Dear ¹**M**____ Yellin,

A Becoming involved in the film industry has been **my ²a**_____ for almost as long as I can remember. Although I have **no ³p**_____ **experience** of film-making, nor had the chance to gain **relevant ⁴q**_____ yet, I believe it is a career that I would **find ⁵f**_____ . I have watched many documentaries on famous directors, which have helped to ⁶**e**_____ **my knowledge** of the field.

B I trust that you will ⁷**c**_____ **my application**, and hope that we may have the ⁸**o**_____ to discuss it ⁹**f**_____ at an interview.

C I was delighted to hear that a film is going to be made in this area, and am writing to **apply for the ¹⁰p**_____ you have advertised.

D In addition to my interest in film-making, I believe that I would be ¹¹**w**_____ **-s**_____ to doing the work you require, as I possess the right ¹²**c**_____ of skills to be of use to you. First of all, my ¹³**s**_____ English is good, which would ¹⁴**e**_____ me to act as an effective interpreter. I am also confident and friendly, so would easily be able to assist you in finding suitable extras for the film. And as for finding locations, I have lived in this area all my life, which makes me ideal for this role. Moreover, I am **a strong team ¹⁵p**_____ , so I am sure that if you hired me, I would fit in quickly and build good relationships with everyone in your film crew.

Yours ¹⁶**f**_____ ,

Jan Barra

1 ____ 2 ____ 3 ____ 4 ____

5 Complete the words (1–16) in Exercise 4. The first letter of each word is given. Is the word for 16 correct?

....

6 Complete the sentences with words or phrases in bold from the sample answer.

  1 I am ...., and I would not let my new colleagues down.

  2 I believe that I have the .... for this position.

  3 I would be very grateful if you would ....

  4 It is .... to work for a small, successful company like yours.

  5 I feel that I would be .... to this position.

  6 The course allowed me to significantly .... of the subject.

  7 Despite the fact that I have .... of this type of work, I am enthusiastic and quick to learn.

  8 I would like to .... of sales assistant in your shop.

  9 Working with children is something I always ....

7 Complete the phrases with one word. Which two are informal?

  1 To .... it may concern:

  2 Dear .... or .... ,

  3 All the .... ,

  4 .... sincerely,

  5 .... Human Resources Manager,

  6 .... there, Sam,

8 Read the question and plan your email of application. What qualities do you have to offer? What might you like to do in the future, and how would the experience of working as a tourist guide help you with this?

> The tourist office in the area where you live is offering the opportunity for someone your age to train as a part-time tourist guide, working at weekends and during the holidays. Write to apply to do the training, explaining why you are suitable for this kind of work and how experience as a tourist guide would help you with your future career ambitions.

....

....

....

 PREPARE FOR THE EXAM

Writing Part 2

9 Write your email of application. Use some of the expressions you have learned. Write 220–260 words.

 EXAM TIP

Imagine that a lot of people will be applying for the same job, so you need to include information that makes you particularly suited to the position – even if you have to invent some of it!

Acknowledgements

Helen Tiliouine wishes to thank Julie Buck for her positive comments and flexibility.

David McKeegan would like to thank editors Julie Buck and Dan Ashton for their help and encouragement.

The authors and publishers acknowledge the following sources of copyright material and are grateful for the permissions granted. While every effort has been made, it has not always been possible to identify the sources of all the material used, or to trace all copyright holders. If any omissions are brought to our notice, we will be happy to include the appropriate acknowledgements on reprinting and in the next update to the digital edition, as applicable.

Key: U = Unit.

Texts
U2: The Guardian for the adapted text from 'It's time to tune in: why listening is the real key to communication' by Kate Murphy, *The Guardian*, 25.1.2020. Copyright © 2021 Guardian News & Media Ltd. Reproduced with permission; **U6:** The Guardian for the adapted text from 'Ship me to Cornwall … a container stay on Bodmin Moor: review' by Dixe Wills, *The Guardian*, 2.7.2016. Copyright © 2021 Guardian News & Media Ltd. Reproduced with permission; **U7:** The Guardian for the adapted text from 'Solar plane makes history after completing round-the-world trip' by Damian Carrington, *The Guardian*, 26.7.2016. Copyright © 2021 Guardian News & Media Ltd. Reproduced with permission; **U9:** The Guardian for the adapted text from 'Fit in your 40s: 'earthquake' workouts are a big timesaver – but do they work?' by Zoe Williams, *The Guardian*, 10.10.2020. Copyright © 2021 Guardian News & Media Ltd. Reproduced with permission; The Guardian for the adapted text from 'Fit in your 40s: 'earthquake' workouts are a big timesaver – but do they work?' by Zoe Williams, *The Guardian*, 12.9.2020. Copyright © 2021 Guardian News & Media Ltd. Reproduced with permission; Australian Broadcasting Corporation for the adapted text from 'Mythbusting Superfoods (presenter Robyn Williams and guest Emma Beckett)' by Robyn Williams and Emma Beckett. Reproduced by permission of the Australian Broadcasting Corporation – Library Sales Ockham's Razor © 2016 ABC; **U10:** The Guardian for the adapted text from 'Juliana Buhring: How cycling round the world saved me' by Rob Penn, *The Guardian*, 15.5.2016. Copyright © 2021 Guardian News & Media Ltd. Reproduced with permission; **U14:** The Guardian for the adapted text from 'A working life: the ice-cream maker' by Mark King, *The Guardian*, 26.8.2011. Copyright © 2021 Guardian News & Media Ltd. Reproduced with permission; **U15:** The Guardian for the adapted text from 'Izzy Christiansen: 'It's really important that we are role models' by Louise Taylor, *The Guardian*, 11.7.2016. Copyright © 2021 Guardian News & Media Ltd. Reproduced with permission.

Photography
The following photographs have been sourced from Getty Images.

U1: vadimguzhva/iStock/Getty Images Plus; SW Productions/Photodisc; -101PHOTO-/iStock/Getty Images Plus; Juanmonino/iStock/Getty Images Plus; Blend Images/Mike Kemp; praetorianphoto/E+; David Madison/DigitalVision; **U2:** Cultura RM Exclusive/Frank and Helena; Chainarong Prasertthai/iStock/Getty Images Plus; Parkpoom Yeesoontes/EyeEm; Kentaroo Tryman/Maskot; Tim Robberts/DigitalVision; **U3:** Man_Half-tube/DigitalVision Vectors; Nastco/iStock/Getty Images Plus; DEA/M. SANTINI/De Agostini; Frank Lennon/Toronto Star; **U4:** ferlistockphoto/iStock/Getty Images Plus; istetiana/Moment; Peathegee Inc; digitalskillet/iStock/Getty Images Plus; Tim Robberts/DigitalVision; Jon Feingersh Photography Inc/DigitalVision; Westend61; fcafotodigital/E+; SDI Productions/E+; Todor Tsvetkov/E+; **U5:** Steve Cicero/Corbis Documentary; kali9/E+; Gpointstudio/Cultura; **U6:** anyaberkut/iStock/Getty Images Plus; James Osmond/The Image Bank; monkeybusinessimages/iStock/Getty Images Plus; slovegrove/iStock Editorial;

U7: © Marco Bottigelli/Moment; Handout/Getty Images News; South_agency/E+; Francesco Carta fotografo/Moment; Westend61; Tim Robberts/Stone; Junior Asiama/500px; adrian825/iStock/Getty Images Plus; nensuria/iStock/Getty Images Plus; **U8:** Pekic/E+; Juanmonino/iStock/Getty Images Plus; Ana Francisconi/EyeEm; Ranta Images/iStock/Getty Images Plus; kali9/iStock/Getty Images Plus; Robert Daly/OJO Images; Andrew Hobbs/The Image Bank; Linka A Odom/Stone; **U9:** Betsie Van Der Meer/Stone; Tim Platt/DigitalVision; PeopleImages/E+; AndreyPopov/iStock/Getty Images Plus; **U10:** Sebastian Bockrandt/EyeEm; Matt_Gibson/iStock/Getty Images Plus; track5/E+; gaspr13/iStock/Getty Images Plus; Betsie Van Der Meer/Stone; **U11:** Nora Carol Photography/Moment; electravk/Moment; Antonio_Diaz/iStock/Getty Images Plus; Maskot; Portra/DigitalVision; SeanShot/E+; **U12:** Westend61Drazen_/E+; Fotoeventis/iStock/Getty Images Plus; Rosemary Calvert/Stone; Alexander Spatari/Moment; **U13:** Emma Kim/Cultura; sturti/E+; f28production/E+; Westend61; Nattakorn Maneerat/iStock/Getty Images Plus; JoeClemson/iStock/Getty Images Plus; tommaso79/iStock/Getty Images Plus; **U14:** Luis Alvarez/DigitalVision; Halfdark; Peter Dazeley/The Image Bank; Vincent Besnault/The Image Bank sanjeri/E+; XiXinXing/iStock/Getty Images Plus; **U15:** Wolfgang Weinhaeupl; Simon Ritzmann/Photodisc; Ridofranz/iStock/Getty Images Plus; Klaus Vedfelt/DigitalVision; **U16:** JohnnyGreig/E+; Tom Chance; Gary John Norman/DigitalVision; alvarez/E+; Justin Case/DigitalVision; LightFieldStudios/iStock/Getty Images Plus; Tim Robberts/Stone; BFC/Ascent Xmedia/Photodisc; Alphotographic/iStock Unreleased.

The following photograph has been sourced from another source.

U11: imageBROKER/Alamy Stock Photo.

Front cover photography by oxygen/Moment/Getty Images.

Audio
Audio production by Leon Chambers at the SoundHouse Studios, London.

Typesetting
Typeset by emc design ltd.